THE LITERARY CLEF

ACKNOWLEDGMENTS

ACKNOWLEDGMENTS are gratefully made to many friends and colleagues who have generously assisted in the compilation of this anthology by offering little-known or unpublished documents. I am indebted to M. Marc Pincherle for permission to include the letters of Edouard Lalo published in *Musiciens peints par eux-mêmes*; to M. Oswald d'Estrade-Guerra and Mlle. Chabrier, officials of the Bibliothèque Nationale, for their tireless efforts in procuring the curious illustrations of Chabrier; to M. Henri Borgeaud for permission to include letters of Debussy to Pierre Louÿs; to the controller of the Debussy estate for other letters of Debussy; to Madame Philippe Fauré-Frémiet for a selection from Fauré's *Lettres intimes* and for the two portraits of Fauré by Sargent; to Madame Marcelle Gérar for permission to include a selection from *Ravel au Miroir de ses Lettres*; and to Madame Valentine Hugo for kindly offering unpublished letters of Erik Satie.

E. L.

Chabrier [1879]
by Edouard Manet

THE LITERARY CLEF

An anthology of letters and writings
by French composers
compiled and translated by

EDWARD LOCKSPEISER

LONDON
JOHN CALDER

PUBLISHED IN GREAT BRITAIN BY
JOHN CALDER (PUBLISHERS) LIMITED
17 SACKVILLE STREET · LONDON · W.1

© JOHN CALDER (PUBLISHERS) LTD. 1958

PRINTED IN GREAT BRITAIN BY
PAGE BROS. (NORWICH) LTD.

CONTENTS

ILLUSTRATIONS

INTRODUCTION

*T*HERE *is nearly always something appealing in letters written by literary people. Whether they are recounting an anecdote or are merely passing on a trivial piece of news one may be sure to find some kind of illumination of the writer's character and, with luck, a link with his work. Biographers in the literary sphere have always looked upon letters and journals as material of the first importance, often the only documentary source which allows them to trace the origin of an artist's work, to watch its growth and to take part in that strange psychological process of an artist's identification with his creations. Such documents are themselves part of literature; some authors, in fact, are better known to us today from some pointed comment in their private diaries or correspondence than from the façade of their completed works.*

The letters of musicians have not quite this interest. One is not likely to learn very much about a composer's musical nature from his account of troubles at a rehearsal, his hagglings with publishers or any other of the bothersome matters a composer has to contend with. Composers are practical-minded men for whom the complexity of a score has the precision of a piece of machinery and who are sometimes required to organise their equally complex careers in a way that demands an almost contrapuntal sense of economics. Lully and Handel, for instance, are composers who, as men, are known to us mainly as hard-headed business executives: the parallels between the inner stresses of their lives and their musical achievement evade us. The mundane details in the correspondence of these remoter figures are nevertheless useful to biographers—content as they have been obliged to be with these meagre gleanings.

With the composers of the nineteenth century, however, it is another matter. The librettos, books, memoirs and correspondence of both

Berlioz and Wagner are themselves outstanding literary accomplishments, quite apart from their musical interest. Writing for these composers was a subsidiary profession. The result is that one can see the interlocking of the man and his work in each of these figures as clearly as in their contemporaries Byron and Bernard Shaw. But the biographer of a musician is not always so fortunate. Portraits of other composers of the period sometimes emerge from their critical writings, but more often from their highly characteristic letters; and particularly, as it seems to me, when a selection is made emphasizing the composer's cast of mind.

In this anthology letters of a group of nineteenth-century French composers have been selected in the hope of providing a key to some aspects of their personalities.   When Berlioz describes his mighty wrestlings with the libretto of The Trojans *or Debussy his sleepless nights in pursuit of the shadowy Mélisande a moving commentary is provided on these operas which we may see gradually taking shape in the composers' minds. When the young Bizet exuberantly writes of the peasant-girls he smothered in flowers at the Roman Carnival or of the wild mobs that went about shooting at random in the streets of Montmartre during the Commune we may see clearly enough the composer of* Carmen. *The prim figure and amiable irony of Saint-Saëns is reflected in quaint accounts of his visits to Victorian England; Fauré offers delicate vignettes of moonlit scenes at Lugano, and Ravel a fantastic picture of fairyland surprisingly inspired by the sight of an iron foundry on the Rhine. Contributions of these and other composers are commented upon in prefatory notes.*

A life-size figure of this period is Emmanuel Chabrier. I fancy that to English readers his letters may be a revelation. A master of racey prose who at his best was something of a cross between Rabelais and Maupassant, Chabrier crammed into his long, rambling letters a wealth of observation, mercilessly accurate in detail, sensitive to sham —he could seldom refrain from dropping into an expressive slang of his own—and hilariously funny. The main French publication of his correspondence (Chabrier d'après ses lettres *by Joseph Désaymard) is as delectable as the music of Chabrier itself.*

It is good to be reminded of the prejudices of nineteenth-century composers. To Fauré Puccini was anathema. And so was most other Italian music. At Cologne he hears a performance of Bellini's Norma which is completely outside his world of experience, a mummified relic, it seems to him, of the forgotten past. In a letter not included in this anthology Debussy hears a work of Busoni which, he says, is as revolting as Richard Strauss. How admirably self-sufficient! As for Brahms, he should be sent back to the class-room, says Lalo, to learn the difference between an oboe and a clarinet. Composers who voiced odd opinions of this sort nowadays would be put down as morons: in our age of historical rummaging a composer must be prepared, chameleon-like, to identify himself with every known style.

The small worlds of certain of these French figures are enchanting still precisely because they were walled round in this way. Beyond the walls were the giants—the giants of Beethoven and Wagner, who have continuously haunted French musical minds and with whom, even in our own time, they have never really come to terms. Readers who may wish to pursue these Franco-German cross-currents are recommended to read Beethoven in France. The Growth of an Idea by Leo Schrade (London, 1942) and Richard Wagner et le Symbolisme français by Grange Woolley (Paris, 1931). Throughout this period two musical civilisations face each other, merge and finally agree upon some kind of tolerable coexistence. It is a fact that no one has written more forcefully about Beethoven than Romain Rolland; and certainly there was never a more ardent Wagnerian than Debussy. But directly critics approach the shattering impact of German Romanticism on French music discussions plunge into abstract realms of philosophical and even religious thought, generally too nebulous, I have thought, for inclusion in this modest anthology.

1957   E.L.

HECTOR BERLIOZ

[1803-1869]

BERLIOZ *wrote volumes of letters, articles and essays in an expansive, virile style. Some kind of fire of the mind illuminates them, as it does his Romantic music. Volumes of Berlioz criticisms have been written too. But the trouble with many of them is that the tenor of their extravagant claims too closely resembles the extravagant and histrionic nature of the debatable genius who was Berlioz himself.*

Berlioz was the great actor of music. In our own day composers have been reluctant to face the glare of public life. Elgar and Debussy are examples of twentieth-century composers who consistently shrank from any suggestion of publicity. In Berlioz's day it was apparently a virtue to be publicity-minded: the more reverberations of Romantic idealism the better. Consequently it is not surprising to find that Berlioz wrote a long biographical tract about himself in the third person (destined for publication by his friend Joseph d'Ortigue in the Revue de Paris).

This biographical sketch, first published by Julien Tiersot and not previously translated into English, was later expanded into the famous Memoirs. Reticence was not part of Berlioz's nature, and as is well-known from his programme for the Symphonic Fantastique, *he had no hesitation in capitalising the most intimate episodes of his courtship of Harriet Smithson. It may be argued that the age of Berlioz never allowed itself to doubt. He was the Byron of music who constantly saw himself in this role. The misunderstood lover informs his public exactly where, in his music, were to be found the pangs of frustration.*

The natural grandiloquence of Berlioz does not falsify this literature. The accounts of his historic meeting with Paganini and of

*the death of Harriet Smithson are moving pages where, for a moment,
we may glimpse the man behind the mask. Equally moving are the
noble pages to the Princess Carolyne Sayn-Wittgenstein where the
daily life of the ageing composer, hard put to scratch a living out of
hack journalism, forms the background of the detailed story he gives
the Princess of the birth of* Les Troyens. *These are inspiring
documents, but one wonders on what sort of ears his erudite discourses
on the Latin poets were to fall. The Princess's letters to Berlioz are
frequently referred to, but only two or three of them are extant and
are not remarkable for any kind of understanding of Berlioz's purpose:
the eccentric Princess was Berlioz's matriarchal figure-head, secretly
dominating him, as Chopin was dominated by George Sand and
Tchaikovsky by Madame von Meck. One is at any rate grateful for
her remoteness since it produced these outpourings on* Les Troyens
*as well as on projects for operas on the subjects of Christopher
Columbus and Cleopatra.*

*An affecting episode, is Berlioz's return at the end of his life to
Estelle Dubœuf (here addressed as Madame Fornier), the innocent
love of his boyhood days, now an aged grandmother enjoying the
peace of her country home. The lovers' meetings evoke an other-
worldly scene almost prophetic of Verlaine's* Colloque *sentimental.
Of this period was the evocative* L'Enfance du Christ. *And one
finds something of the same quiet dignity in Berlioz's solicitude for
the welfare of the ageing lady who was ultimately left by the chastened
composer with a modest bequest.*

BERLIOZ

BIOGRAPHICAL SKETCH WRITTEN BY THE COMPOSER.[1]

HECTOR BERLIOZ was born at La Côte St André (Isère) on December 11th 1803. His father intended that he should follow the medical profession in which he had himself achieved distinction. At all events, and simply from a desire to complete his education, he procured a music master for the boy when he was twelve or thirteen. At the end of six months the young Berlioz was able to sing at sight and play the flute reasonably well. His dislike for physiology only became greater the nearer the time came for him to take up these studies seriously.

His father had the following idea for winning him over. Setting out on his table the great treatise on osteology by Monro, with its life-size plates, he would call in his son and, showing him the picture of death, would say: "Hector, these are subjects that we might study together. Come now, if you agree to begin straight away I shall have an excellent flute fitted with all the new keys brought for you from Paris." The unfortunate child, walking into the trap, promised everything his father asked for and then ran off to lock himself up in his room when he wept long and bitterly.

However, beguiled as he was by his father's affectionate concern for his welfare, he pursued these studies, taken up so unwillingly, for two years under his father's guidance.

But he was already possessed by the musical demon; he spent sleepless nights gazing at harmony books he was unable to understand; he made futile attempts at composition which were

---

[1] The manuscript of this sketch is in Paris Conservatoire Library. It is published in Julien Tiersot's *Lettres de Musiciens écrites en Francais*, Vol. II. The sketch was utilised by Joseph d'Ortigue in an article in *La Revue de Paris*, 1832.

7

entrusted to the amateur musicians of La Côte St André, there to be greeted with laughter and jeers.

The meaning of harmony was ultimately revealed to him quite spontaneously by a quartet of Haydn. Merely by listening to it, reading it and copying it out in score, Berlioz grew to understand the mysteries of chords and from this moment grasped all that had eluded him in perusing so much didactic rubbish. He immediately composed a Quintet for flute, two violins, viola and bass which, far from being booed, was warmly applauded by its performers. This success began to cause his father some concern.

Shortly after, Berlioz came to Paris to complete his distasteful studies at the Medical School. He became acquainted with the anatomy theatre and also with the Opéra. Caught thus between death and passion, between the sight of horrifying corpses and ravishingly beautiful *danseuses*, between the music of Gluck on the one hand and, on the other, the prose of Bichat, he nevertheless kept for a year the promise he had made to his father to follow his classes regularly, encouraged as he was by his fellow-student M. Robert who is today one of the most distinguished young surgeons.

However, he frequently disturbed the peace of the anatomy theatre by impassioned accounts of a performance he had just heard, and while sawing or hammering away at a skull he would chant the beautiful melodies from *La Vestale* or from *Cortez*.

The following year the anatomist-musician wrote to his father to the effect that he could no longer resist his calling for art nor his dislike of medicine; he asked him to agree to his changing his plans for he foresaw that the life he had so far been leading would be in complete disharmony with his nature.

Berlioz's parents thereupon began a series of set-tos with their son which lasted almost four years, the only result of which was to upset all the members of the family, none of whom would abandon his particular viewpoint.

Nothing was left undone to bring him back to what they called the right way. Entreaties, threats, the cutting off of his allowance, cajolings and promises, even curses—all these failed, faced with Berlioz's will of iron and his great musical passion.

His father having in a fit of despair written that he would yield no more and that henceforth he must depend on himself, Berlioz applied to the director of the Théâtre des Nouveautés, which was then being built, asking for a post as flautist in the orchestra.

"No posts for flautists, they are all taken."

"Engage me then as a chorus-singer."

"Monsieur, the ranks in the chorus are all accounted for, I can see no way of employing you. . . . But wait a minute, we might just need a bass in the chorus. Leave your address."

Some days later Berlioz was requested to call at the management of the theatre. There was to be a competition for the post of chorus-singer.

Among his rival competitors were a blacksmith, a weaver, a chorister from St Eustache and a former singer at the *Panorama dramatique*. They each sang a piece of their choice. Then came Berlioz's turn.

"Well, Monsieur, what have you brought?"

"Nothing. Have you not any music here?"

"No, none at all."

"What! Not even an Italian vocal exercise?"

"No indeed. In any case I fancy you do not sing at sight?"

"You will allow me to say that I will sing anything you like at sight."

"Ah, that's a different matter. I imagine then that you must know some operatic aria."

"Yes, sir, I know by heart the entire operatic repertoire—*La Vestale*, *Cortez*, *Oedipe*, *Les Danaïdes*, the two *Iphigénies*, *Orphée*, *Armide*. . . ."

"Enough, enough. Good Lord, what a memory! Since you

pretend to be so clever, sing us then the great aria from the third act of *Oedipe* with the recitative."

Berlioz sang the aria asked of him, accompanied only by a violin which here and there struck up a few chords. The candidates were dismissed. The next day Berlioz received a letter from the management informing him that he had triumphed over the blacksmith, the weaver, the chorister from St Eustache even over the singer of the *Panorama dramatique*, and that he was engaged as a chorister at the Théâtre des Nouveautés at a salary of fifty francs a month. He held this post for three months. After this, tired of shrieking out the blaring Vaudeville tunes and having found some theory pupils who provided him with a means of existence, he left the theatre to complete, in solitude, the opera *Les Francs Juges* which has never been performed but of which the overture is now famous. His parents, impressed by his perseverance, reinstated the modest allowance which they had withdrawn.

For a moment he was happy enough, but he was approaching the event which was about to change his entire life. It is difficult to imagine what love must mean to a soul such as the soul of Berlioz. He was himself unaware of the fact that there comes a time in life when the intensity of one's passions reaches a degree making all earlier feelings appear pale and insignificant. This lesson he learnt from a famous Irishwoman. An English theatrical company had displayed to us in Paris the wonders of Shakespeare's genius. An actress unrecognised in England played the role of Ophelia in *Hamlet* and was greeted with a remarkable and well-deserved success. Berlioz saw her and from that moment on he was completely overcome by a sudden, inexplicable love of terrifying violence and persistence. All attempts to find love requited being in vain, he sank into the most pitiful state of despair. He wrote no more music, he couldn't even listen to music, the things he usually admired offering to him, in this heartbroken state, nothing but intolerable suffering.

Berlioz [1832] by Emile Signol

Three Caricatures
of Berlioz

Right: [1831] by
Horace Vernet

Below left: [1855] by
Joseph Mollard

Below right: [1847] by
an anonymous artist

He was to be seen in the corner of the orchestra pit at the Odéon, when the English troupe was not playing (for he would have been extremely moved at the thought of seeing Miss S. again), pale of face, unkempt, his long hair and his beard dishevelled, listening quietly to some comedy or other of Picard which now and again would bring forth from him a sudden burst of laughter like the sudden and wild laughter of a person who has been mercilessly tickled. Some of the artists took pity on him, but others who used to call him *Père la Joie* merely made fun of him.

"Oh, the unfortunate creature," he would exclaim. "If only she could for a moment understand a love like mine, she would throw herself into my arms even though she were to perish from my embraces."

Often, after fifteen months' absence from the beautiful Islander, when Berlioz's friends, aware of his calmer demeanour, hoped to bring him back to a normal way of living—his recollections of her having in the meantime seemingly faded—he was to be seen suddenly stopping short in the midst of some merry conversation, his pale face covered in perspiration. His whole being would then tremble violently and he would let forth a flood of tears.

One day, in the course of the third year of this passionate state of mind, Berlioz, having heard Miss S. shamefully slandered by a friend, disappeared from Paris for two days. This rash person, who had broken Berlioz's heart with this gossip, had not found him at his home late that evening and was greatly disturbed. They searched for him throughout the town, even at the mortuary, but not a trace. Later he recounted that walking he knew not where, he had gone beyond the city's boundaries and at midnight found himself in the middle of fields near some village quite unknown to him. Unable to proceed any further and overcome with despair, he threw himself on some wheatsheaves where he spent the night not in sleeping or even weeping, but in listening in a state of utter

B

listlessness to the tinkling bells of the cattle herds, the dogs barking at the farm and the chatter of waggoners along the road; and suddenly he laughed out loud at the fright he had given the partridges who in the moonlight had come to peck around his feet.

The next day, wandering on without food, he found himself in a field near Sceaux and then fell exhausted into a ditch where he slept like a log until evening.

Back in Paris by the middle of the night, to the great astonishment of the people about, who believed him to be dead, he refused to utter a word in reply to the many solicitous questions that were put to him. Six months later the *Symphonie Fantastique* was written. Miss S. recently attended Berlioz's concert and avidly read the printed description of the work. She must have experienced a host of strange feelings in realising the harm she was causing this fiery spirit in thus attending the performance of the astonishing work she had inspired, in witnessing the brilliant success of the man she had disdained and in perceiving how this work was in effect a clever revenge. All of this, all these events which occurred quite accidentally make our biography appear to be a novel. This biography is, however, true as those who know Berlioz are only too well aware.

The *Grand Prix* for composition which he was awarded at the French Institute at the time of the three days of the July Revolution, whilst shooting and the wild uproars of the people could be heard in the streets below; his journey to Italy and his near wreck in the Gulf of Genoa on the way to Livorno; his flights into the mountains of the Kingdom of Naples with a gun slung over his shoulder, virtually living on what he was able to hunt and frequenting the haunts of bandits; his spending of whole days in building pyramids of stone on the rocky spit of Subiaco; or at other times lazing in the sunshine like a Neapolitan lazybones and smoking one cigar after another, or throwing himself completely dressed into the Anio, knowing that he might catch his death from fever within three hours; his wild gaiety alternating with a taciturn, brutish mood according to whether he was troubled or not by his Irish memories; his wild admiration at Florence on reading Shakespeare's *King Lear* for the first time; his momentary passion for a Florentine lady who was unknown to him and whom in fact he knew only as a corpse, having kissed the dead lady's hand during the funeral service at the Duomo and bursting then into tears as he followed her procession to the grave—all these various anecdotes suggest at least a great romance of Byron.

* * *

TO HUMBERT FERRAND

January 2nd 1839

Dear Friend,

. . . Yes, yes, it is all true, absolutely true. I imagine you must have seen, since you last wrote to me, the article of Janin and several others, no doubt.

For some time Paganini has made it known that he was one of my staunchest supporters. His attitude was clear from his enthusiasm at the first performance of *Benvenuto*. Then, after my second concert, which I conducted, he came to see me, took my by the arm, led me on to the stage of the Conservatoire just as the musicians were leaving and there he went down on his knees before me. I thought I was dreaming. As you know the poor man has completely lost his voice and so it was his charming little son (who knows him best) who told me what he wanted to say. Paganini heard then my *Harold* Symphony, which is dedicated to you, for the first time. And this was the work which caused this outburst. Two days later, on Tuesday morning, I returned to bed as a result of my bronchitis. Little Achilles came to my room and delivered a letter from his father to which, he said, there was no reply and off he went. Thinking that it was a letter of congratulation, I opened it. You can imagine what I felt on reading the first sentence:

Beethoven spento non c'era che Berlioz che potesse farlo revivere, and enclosed was a 20,000 franc note. At that moment Harriet came in and seeing me in tears, thought that there must be another unfortunate love-affair.

"Come now, what is it? What is the trouble? Take courage."

"It is not a question of trouble; I have a letter from Paganini. And do you know what he has sent me? Twenty thousand francs."

"God, is that possible?" The letter is translated for her; and then running to fetch my little son, "Louis," she says, "come here, come and thank God with me for what He has done for your father." Whereupon mother and child go down on bended knees by my bedside. I am sure you will appreciate this scene.

Four days later, when I was able to go out, there was to be another scene of this kind at the home of Paganini. I went to the Néothermes, where he was living, and there he was alone walking about his billiard room. As his apartment is at the back and quiet, Paganini was able to make himself heard. There was first of all a silence of some five minutes or so whilst we embraced each other and wept copiously. Then, as I was about to speak, Paganini stopped me:

"Say not a word, I am overcome with joy, this is the greatest satisfaction I have had in my life. You have opened up to me a new realm of feeling and I could do nothing less for a man such as you."

Then, drying his eyes and bringing down his fist on to the billiard table, he burst out laughing: "Ha, ha, ha! I am happy, happy indeed to think that all those wretches who have been writing and talking against you will not now be so impudent. For they are aware that I know what I am talking about and that I am not an easy person."

Paganini left last week for Marseilles and these were his last words on leaving me: "Adieu . . . aimez-moi!" I shall write to him shortly and shall write a new symphony for him.

I shall not tell you of the impression produced by this tremendous act. My friends are triumphant, those that were on the borderline are rallying, my enemies are furious and vainly attempt to misrepresent this fine gesture of a great artist whom they are either unable or do not wish to understand. The English press is wonderful, they have made a terrific affair of it in London. . . .

You have no idea of the magnificence of this last concert, the performance surpassed everything. There were unbelievable effects, not only in the hall where women were to be seen sobbing, but from the orchestra, one of the first violins being obliged to leave overcome with emotion. As for myself, I remained unmoved and stood there, amongst all this, like a rock. The rehearsal the day before and the scene from Gluck's *Alceste* had taken the edge off my sensitiveness. . . .

TO ADELE BERLIOZ

March 6th 1854

Harriet died on March 3rd. Louis came to spend four days with us and left for Calais last Wednesday. Fortunately she was able to see him. I had left her a few hours before her death and went in to her room ten minutes after; without pain or the slightest stirring, she had breathed her last breath.

The last rites took place yesterday. I had to look after everything myself—the arrangements at the town hall and the cemetery, and today I am greatly moved. Her state was frightful. Besides paralysis, she was afflicted with erysipelas and could breathe only with great difficulty. She had become a shapeless mass of flesh—and by her side there was the radiant portrait of herself which I had given her last year where you see her as she was with her large thoughtful eyes. She has gone. My friends have rallied. A large number of literary figures and artists led by Baron Taylor accompanied the coffin to the cemetery at Montmartre near our bereaved house. The sun shone brilliantly over the plain of Saint-Denis but I hadn't the heart to follow the procession; I stayed in the garden.

I had been too overcome the day before when I went to call on the Pastor, M. Haussmann, who lives in the Faubourg St Germain. By one of those terrible coincidences my carriage had to pass by the Théâtre de l'Odéon where I had seen her for the first time twenty-seven years ago when she had at her feet the élite of the Paris world. There was the Odéon which had caused me so much anguish: we could neither live together nor leave each other and during the last ten years of our life we were aware of this frightful dilemma. We caused each other so much suffering! I have come from the cemetery now and am alone. She lies on the side of the hill facing the north, looking towards England where she never wished to return.

I wrote to poor Louis yesterday, and shall write to him again.

How dreadful life is! My mind is crowded with memories, sweet and bitter intertwined: her wonderful qualities, her demands, her unreasonableness, her genius and her misfortunes. Frightful, dreadful! It was she who revealed Shakespeare to me and the wonders of drama. She suffered with me in poverty, she never hesitated to risk our wherewithal for the sake of some musical venture. But then in contrast to this courageous outlook, she was always opposed to my leaving Paris, she would never allow me to travel. If I had not taken extreme measures I should still be today almost unknown in Europe. And then there was her jealousy, her unfounded jealousy which eventually became the reason for the entire change in my life.

My dear sister, I should so much like to see you. But this is not possible. In a month's time I shall return to Germany. I am engaged to perform at Dresden, the Intendant of the King of Saxony wrote to me yesterday and they are expecting me. I have no feeling for anything, music or anything else. I have kept her hair. Here I am in this big salon next to her own deserted room. The garden is breaking into bud. If only I could forget, forget! . . . How can I be rid of my memories, how can these feelings be torn from my heart? Life is indeed long; and already Louis has grown up, he is no longer the dear child I would watch running along the garden paths. I have here a daguerrotype of him taken at the age of twelve. I have the impression that that child is lost to me. . . .

Do not be amazed at these thoughts of mine; I could tell you many more of this kind. How easy but fatal to recall the past! Which is why I have been afflicted with the cruel success of recalling such impressions in certain of my works. . . .

TO THE PRINCESS CAROLYNE SAYN-WITTGENSTEIN

March 1852

Madame,

Liszt has afforded me great pleasure in persuading you to send me such a gracious letter. I am most suceptible to the compliment. The account it contains allows me to judge the vexations, obstacles and absurdities of all kinds that my excellent friend must have experienced, suffered and surmounted to reach the goal he set himself.

I am sure you must often have given him support in this struggle, so little deserved by a man such as he, and that he accepted it from you only because of his true feelings of friendship. I have no illusions about my own debt to you. I offer you, Madame, my sincere gratitude.

Liszt's behaviour in this matter, so strikingly idealistic, has been the admiration of all enlightened minds, the admiration too of all artistic souls, friends and enemies. The stupid seek a *reason* which of course they will never find.

In following the valuable advice which you kindly gave me, I am enclosing a letter to the Grand Duchess which I beg Liszt to present to Her Highness. I will certainly do all I can to reach Weimar by the end of the year and to thank personally all those who have shown me such interest and kindness. I trust Liszt will allow me to present my first respects to yourself. . . .

1855 *or* 1856

Dear Princess,

I saw M. de Calonne recently. The article has been set up and de Calonne assures me he will send a proof to Liszt. What a business! And what a waste of time! All these goings and comings for something that should have been done in five days. Some people appear to be born to live two hundred years by the way they go about things. I am delighted that you are pleased with the choice of photographs, but it is not I who deserve your thanks for they were chosen by your nephew. I was in bed when they were sent. I imagine that the Sax instruments have at last arrived.

I see that the Berlin critics are flogging again the dead horse of the religious paradox in music: materialistic music, passionate music, dramatic music, fashionable music—they want a Christian to pray as a statue would pray if it could speak. But the real reason for their attitude is one that I have frequently mentioned, namely they want religious music to be devoid of melody, harmony, rhythm, expression, orchestral colour and a sense of tonality because once you admit all this anyone can write marvellous music of this kind.

And these same fellows who find modern religious music bogus in feeling, who refer to it as "materialist" music, have not a word to say about the platitudinous rubbish and the distortions of those countless dramatic works with which Europe is nowadays flooded. Bogus standards in music are the only ones that count! Paradise will certainly have to be a tremendous place to accommodate all the fools who believe they are going there. . . .

You have no doubt heard of the terrible things that are happening on Thalberg's visit to Buenos Aires. Women simply faint when they hear him; I can at any rate vouch for the fate of Madame Hans who, said the local correspondent, was carried home dead. But now they say she is getting better; she may be saved! . . . So much wild publicity is going about, you hardly dare face the mention of Thalberg's name. Alternatively we must improve upon this publicity and declare that at one of his concerts men killed each other, that the effect of his playing was such that women who were not pregnant gave birth to children or that the whole audience was literally thunderstruck and electrified.

Meyerbeer has put out a statement that for some weeks he has been suffering from toothache. How would it be if I were to proclaim that Liszt was not suffering from toothache? Many people who are afraid of his bite might think again.

Truly, Princess, I fear that I am imposing upon your kindness in allowing me to indulge in follies of this kind—or perhaps you have not allowed me? But this question of fashionable religious music makes me wince, it sets my teeth on edge. They make no distinction between the bad cheap style and the real thing. Raphael and Michelangelo have thus committed real crimes in religious painting by using rich palettes. They should have kept to black and white. Also their virgins, their saints are too expressive, too lifelike! (I can imagine that the Italians, according to this theory, might begin to extol their achievements in the *Commedia dell' Arte!*).

What then should we do? What should we say? Nothing? Remain quiet? Never in your life. Provide us with double-edged hatchets and let us strike right and left and on to the wounds let us pour the burning dust of ridicule. There will be at least some satisfaction in that. If idiocy is immortal let it at any rate be deformed and ugly. I await a detailed letter from Liszt on Berlin and this Berlinism.

The Baron von Wangenheim has just written to me informing me of the concert at Gotha on February 6th. . . . I shall send you a list of the dead and wounded women. . . .

Forgive me, Princess, in my next letter I shall be only pompous, frigid, colourless and conventional.

Your devoted

H. B.

May 17th 1856

Dear Princess,

I have many apologies to make; I am ashamed at not yet having replied to your fine encouraging letter. I wanted to be able to say something definite on the great enterprise of which you are the prime cause. I finished the verses of the first act [of *Les Troyens*] only the day before yesterday; this will be the longest act of all and I spent ten days on it from May 5th to the 15th. These were my only completely free days since my return from Weimar. I shall not describe the various phases of discouragement, joy, disgust, pleasure and fury through which I have successively passed during these ten days. Twenty times I was on the point of throwing the whole thing on the fire and giving myself over to a life of contemplation. Now I am certain not to lack the courage to bring the work to its conclusion: I am held by it. Also from time to time I read your letter to spur me on. Normally I was disheartened towards the evening but returned to the charge in the morning while the day was young. Now I hardly sleep at all. I am thinking of it all the time, and if I had the time to work, in two months the whole of this mosaic would be completed. But how can I do that? I must busy myself with my candidature at the Institute, consult everybody and anybody (and many nobodies), run about Paris from morning till night; and constantly I have some devil of an article to write about some new instrumentalist or singer, a revival of some old opera or even the first performance of an old opera, some concert with which I am behind-hand, the memory of which suddenly bursts in upon your days like the last rocket at a firework display burning the beards of a few stray passers-by.

In regard to the music, I shall need a good year and a half, I calculate (as the Americans say), to lay it out. It will be a large construction; let us hope that it will be built from fired and not from unfired bricks like the Palaces of Nineveh. Unless they are baked, bricks soon turn to mud and dust. . . .

I receive no letters from anyone; and no one replies to mine.
. . . Adieu, Princess, you will reply for the shade of Virgil one
of these nights and for the outrages that I have committed on
his great lines—especially if my Palace is made of unfired brick
and if the hanging gardens are planted only with willows and
wild plum-trees.

June 24th [1856]

Forgive me, I beg you, Princess, for not having replied to
your two last letters until today. You will have guessed that the
Aeneid and the Academy are the two reasons; but the *Aeneid*
much more than the Academy. Every morning as I went off in
my carriage carrying along with me my notebook, my thoughts
were not for what I was going to say to one of the "Immortals"
of the Academy, but for what my characters were going to say.

Now at last these two troubles are over. The Academy has
nominated me, as you already know; and the opera is almost
finished. I am on the last scene of the 5th Act. I am stirred by
the subject more than I should be and I am resisting temptations
of working on the music. I want the libretto to be completely
settled before starting the score. I couldn't however fail last
week to set down the music for the Duet of Shakespeare:

In such a night as this
When the sweet wind did gently kiss the trees, etc.

And the music for this love story is finished. But I shall want
another fortnight to polish, prune, correct and finally hammer
into shape all these lines as they are now. I tell you thus how
my work is progressing, for assuredly I should never have
undertaken it without your encouragement. . . .

So you see I am now a respectable personage; I am no longer
a vagrant, nor a Bohemian, nor do I expect miracles to happen.
What a game! One day I might even become the Pope! Never
mind, in three weeks I shall have finished scribbling out my

libretto and shall start on the score and shall not let go of it, thinking no more of the Opéra—*quoi qu'il arrive ou qu'il advienne*—than if it didn't exist.

July 1856

Dear Princess,

Of course it is possible, and the manuscript would have been with you before now had I not feared your disappointment with it.

However you must know sooner or later what this amateur poetry of mine looks like, and I shall obey you. Within two or three days *Les Troyens* will be sent off by rail. Be good enough to return the manuscript as soon as possible and let only such good friends of yours see it on whose discretion you may count. I refer to this work as *Les Troyens*, but this is not to say I have finally decided on this title. At the moment it is the one that seems to suit the work best. All the others which I have thought of, *Enée, L'Enéide, Didon, Troie et Carthage, Italie!* were in turn rejected by the few people to whom I have been able to read my work.

This however is not my trouble. My concern now is with the music; and you will be able to judge what an enormous cast the libretto provides for. . . .

You laugh at my idea of retiring, of living in the wilderness and so forth. The fact is that over the last week I have not had a single hour with a clear head to think over my work and that I shall be torn to shreds during the whole of the next month with all sorts of troublesome business.

But then. . . . Well now, will you believe that I have fallen in love, and irretrievably, with my Queen of Carthage? I am simply madly in love with this beautiful Dido. You will find many borrowings from Shakespeare amidst the poetry of Virgil; I've watered down my Cyprian wine with *eau-de-vie*. I should like Rachel Felix to be good enough to read me one of these days the 5th Act, and the scenes of Cassandra in the first and second acts. There are certain points of emphasis, certain moments of silence and certain vocal inflections to be decided upon. But perhaps she is too much the *Diva* and just now the *Diva furens*. The great success of Adelaide Ristosi has caused her to cultivate an emotional intensity which has resulted in her being unapproachable. . . .

Baden, August 12th 1856

How to thank you, Princess, for the kindness which has inspired you to send me such a precious letter! With what perception you have entered into the spirit of these ideas!

You wished to encourage me—I am not mistaking the meaning of what you say: you are now crediting me with the beauties of Virgil's poetry and are even praising my Shakespearian plagiarisms. I shall have the courage to go on to the end, do not fear; it wasn't necessary to inveigh me with praise to which I am not in fact due. The beauties are the beauties of Virgil; the drama is the drama of Shakespeare. Of this I am aware. I am nothing but a plunderer, a filcher of the minds of these two geniuses; and what I have gathered is a wreath of flowers to form a bed for music which, God willing, may not itself perish from their potent perfumes.

Liszt is quite right in saying that the word *Italie* sounds less well than *Italiam* with its accent on the second syllable. But I am writing in French. I had even used the two Latin words *Votum* and *Peplum* but I was advised to replace them by the corresponding French words.

I am also going to go over the Scene of Ascanius who should really not say: "O reine sur nos pas une sanglante trace". That is the reply of a child. But he will reply with the words: "Je suis son fils!", his childish pride containing itself no longer after Panthea has said: "Notre chef est Enée!" As for the scene between Dido and her sister, where you appear to think that the Queen was speaking of Aeneas ahead of time, I cannot understand your mistake. And I was on the point of being vexed with you for having attributed to me such a colossal absurdity. Doubtless the Queen would have to have been lynx-eyed to perceive on a stormy night the Trojan leader on board his vessel. But there was never any question of this; I hadn't even thought of it. It was a mirage of love that I had in mind, so as not to use once more the dream scenes of classical operas. Dido is prey to an insomnia similar to that which Bernardin de St Pierre so well described in *Paul et Virginie*; she is dreaming at the top of the tower of her palace, baring her head and bosom aflame with passion to the blasts of the storm. Then her ardent love strikes a shudder in her soul, she believes she sees from afar a lordly stranger appear, but it is a delusion. In truth she has seen nothing, and she is aware that she has seen nothing:

> Perdue en mes pensées, au sommet de la tour,
> Je *croyais* voir au loin, etc. . . .
>   Mon être tout entier
> Sur des ailes de flamme
> *Semblait* voler à lui.
>
> Jusqu'au lever du jour,
> En proie à cette *illusion*,
> J'ai versé de brûlantes larmes,
> Sans pouvoir me soustraire aux charmes
> De la cruelle *vision*.

So you see that she has neither seen nor did she believe she saw the stranger, and that there is no question of Aeneas.

In regard to another misreading which has caused you to credit me with an idea I never had, I am distressed that here is praise which I do not merit. I refer to the Tomb of Achilles. Your idea is admirable, for the Trojan people were afraid of the Tomb of the Hero. In my version they express fear of the site where he pitches his tent; which in a way corresponds to Virgil

Hic sævus tendebat Achilles. Only in Virgil the Trojan crowd are
not a lot of braggarts.

Thank you, then, for the kindness of heart which has inspired you to encourage me. On my return to Paris I shall
endeavour to free myself from all other business and begin my
musical task. It will be an arduous task; and I pray that the gods
of Virgil will be with me—or I am lost. What is going to be
tremendously difficult is to find the musical *form*, for without
form music simply does not exist, or is merely the humiliated
slave of words.

This is the crime of Wagner; he wants to dethrone music, to
reduce its function to the marking of expressive accents, thereby
exaggerating the ideas of Gluck (who most fortunately did not
himself succeed in following his ungodly theory). I am for that
music which you yourself call free. Yes, free, proud, supreme,
masterly—I want it to embrace everything, to assimilate everything, to be music that shall transcend the Alps and the Pyrenees. But to achieve such conquests, it must fight its own battles,
it cannot rely on subordinates; I agree that music should make
use of good poetry, but like Napoleon it must face the fire
itself, like Alexander it must itself march in the front rank, of
the army. . . . To attempt to bring music back to the
measured rhythms of classical choruses is an example of the
most unbelievable, and fortunately the most useless stupidity
in the history of art. . . .

Another danger that besets me in composing the music for
this drama is in the fact that the feelings I am called upon to
express are inclined to move me too deeply. This can bring the
whole matter to nought. Passionate subjects must be dealt with
in cold blood. This is what held me back so much in writing
the adagio of *Roméo et Juliette* and the reconciliation scene in
the last movement. I thought I should never come to grips with
it.

Time, time—that is our greatest master! Alas, like Ugolino,
time devours its own children. . . .

Paris, November 14th 1856

I have not stopped my Phrygian task for a day despite those moments of dejection caused by my indisposition. I found then all that I had written cold, flat, silly and insipid. I had a mind to burn the lot.

The human mind is very strange and unfathomable. Now that I am better I have read my score over again and find that it is by no means so worthless as I thought.

I am still at the big ensemble:

> *Châtiment effroyable!*
> *Mystérieuse horreur!*

after Aeneas has recounted the catastrophe of Laocoon. It takes me two days, sometimes only one, to write a section, but then I require three weeks to think it over, to turn it into shape and to orchestrate it.

The libretto too is being changed a little. I have just added another scene to the first act. It will not lengthen the act for it will take the place of a ballet scene during the popular re-joicings that take place, if you remember, in the plain before Troy. The whole Trojan population, the Army led by Aeneas, Priam, the Queen, Helen, the Princes and Princesses, the Trojan children led by Ascanius, the people and the priests, form a procession to offer a sacrifice to Jupiter and Neptune for the deliverance of Troy. I thought that one of the most moving figures in this episode should similarly appear in the course of this ceremonial. Accordingly, after the various state corporations have placed their offerings at the country altar, and at the moment when the celebrations reach their climax, the music suddenly changes and to the air of a tearful and (if possible) heartbreaking mimed dance Andromache comes forward hand in hand with Astyanax who carries a basket of flowers. They are in white (the ancient colour of mourning) and kneel in silence before the altar. The child offers his basket of flowers whilst the mother prays; she then presents her son to Priam who blesses him. She is unable to withhold her tears, she lowers her veil, takes Astyanax by the hand once more and they go out slowly without saying a word and return to Troy.

Cassandra, whose appearances are like those of a wounded lioness, perceives Andromache at the back of the stage and says:

Garde tes pleurs, veuve d'Hector,
N'en taris pas la source. Hélas, tu dois encore
A de prochains malheurs bien des larmes amères!

And the Trojan women in chorus reply:

Andromaque et son fils! les épouses, les mères
Pleurent à leur aspect! O destin! ces clameurs
De la publique allégresse!
Et cette immense tristesse,
Et ces gémissements, et ces nobles douleurs!

These eight lines will be sung, or better recited on their own during the performance of the mimed air. Then the celebrations will be resumed. I have gone over this in many places, and I am still working at it; I have taken parts out, added to it and changed it.

An article which I had to finish for today has interrupted me, and I shall have another which will cut across my work tomorrow. It will be like this all the time. . . .

January 7th 1859

A thousand thanks, Princess, on my bended knees for your indulgent letter. Let me kiss the hand—*la mana pietosa*, we have not this adjective in French—that wrote it. I am suffering greatly and I am much moved by the messages of sympathy I receive, yours especially. You allow me to be my stupid self in writing to you. Alas, I shall in any case not need your permission. The doctors say that I have a general inflammation of the system of the "nervous tree", that I shall have to live like an oyster

C

and not think nor react to anything. (It would be nearer the truth to say that I should have to die). The nervous tree, if there is such a tree, produces some very bitter fruit. Imagine that there are days when I am as hysterical as a young girl. The least thing then brings about strange occurrences. The day before yesterday I was quietly talking with some friends by the fireside when I was brought a newspaper in which I saw the announcement of a new biography of Christopher Columbus. Immediately the whole life of this great man was revealed as a single structure to my mind; I saw it as one's eye takes in the whole scene of a picture. The recollection of the famous epic wrung my heart and I fell into a state of indescribable despair, to the amazement of those around me. It was all put down to my state of health. I was not going to let myself be jeered at by declaring my passion for Columbus, the very mention of whose name brought about this crisis. Here was an entanglement of cause and effect in which the most learned physiologists helped by the greatest psychologists would lose their way and be all at sea.

But enough of sickness and the sick man. Your letter, *pietosa* as I must describe it, Liszt's letter which I had earlier, and Madame Viardot whom I saw recently, have given me news of your life at Weimar. I see you at Altenburg, I hear your interesting conversation during the evening enlivened by the sweet smile of the Princess Marie . . . and I begin to think (despite my doctor's advice), and I am comforted by the fact that in this corner of the world in which you live, there is a heart and a mind and noble ideas which you kindle and keep alive.

How I should listen to you, how I should drink in your words and those of Liszt, who says such magnificent things when he speaks of matters that move and inflame him! They want to send me to Cannes, to the Mediterranean sun. If I were free I should choose to go to Weimar. In truth life moves softly over one in the south, the heart expands and imagination takes flight. You would allow me to reflect in my deep chair, to overhear your words or, if I wished, to keep silent. But so many well-wishers bid me remain where I am that I shall obey, like the Wandering Jew.

Nothing new to tell you from the ancient world. Cassandra is stirring and lightning darts from her black eyes. Dido is languishing still, and the beautiful Anna Soror seems to have guessed the sad future of Carthage. The trembling Aeneas obeys the call of the Gods. . . .

June 20th 1859

As for our *Troyens*, I've said not a word, not taken a step nor seen the meanest employee on its behalf. I have again and again licked it into shape like a bear with its cubs. The piano score is finished; and from time to time I have an act or two of it played to see how everything fits in. It will be very difficult for those two great characters Cassandra and Dido; the main point is that the big scenes should be very clearly enunciated, or the whole of the epic passion of these scenes will go for nothing.

I wish you to be assured, Princess, of my gratitude for your determination in my undertaking and completing this work. Whatever its fate may be I am today supremely happy at having completed it. I am now able to judge it quite objectively and I think I may say that the score contains pages worthy of being offered to you. It has some novel devices. The second act contains, for instance, the chorus of Trojan women built on this strange scale:

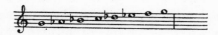

and the effect of desolation resulting from the continual predominance of the G as against the D flat is indeed strange. By this means I have been able to portray the desperate uproar of

the *feminæ ululantes* of Virgil; and the effect is no more un-
couth than of a dishevelled Niobe. The narration of the catastrophe of Laocoon and particularly the ensemble that follows
it are, as I see them, two far-flung scenes of horror that may
strike at your heart. As for the main object of the work, the
expression of passion and feeling, and the musical delineation
of the characters, this had always been my simplest task. I
have spent my life with these demi-gods. I fancy that they know
me as well as I know them. And I recall in this connection a
memory of my childhood which shows how these beautiful
creatures of antiquity have always held a fascination for me.
When I was engaged upon my classical studies I was required
to comment, under my father's guidance, on the twelfth book
of the *Aeneid*. My mind was set afire by the characters of
this masterpiece—Lavinia, Turnus, Aeneas, Mezentius, Lausus,
Pallas, Evander, Amata, Latinus, Camilla and many others.
I went about like a somnambulist and, in the words of
Hugo:

Je marchais tout vivant dans mon rêve étoilé.

One Sunday I was taken to Vespers. The sad, monotonous
chant of the Psalm, *In exitu Israel*, produced on me the magnetic
effect that it does still today and filled me with dreams of the
past. I was at one with my Virgilian heroes, I heard the clash
of their arms, I saw the flight of the beautiful Amazon Camilla,
I was filled with awe at the shameful blushes of the weeping
Lavinia, and the wretched Turnus, and his father Daunus and
his sister Juterna; I heard echoes of the great palaces of Laurentia
and I was overcome by the most terrible grief. I writhed, left
the church in tears and was unable to restrain myself for the
rest of the day, but I never confessed what had thus moved me,
and my parents were never able to imagine what had seized
my young heart.

Is not this one of the strangest and one of the most wonderful
signs of the power of genius? A poet dead for thousands of
years striking at the soul of a simple unknowing child by

means of a story handed down over the centuries and by means of these visions undimmed by time.

I have often wondered what the aim might be of this hoax called Life. The aim is to know the beautiful; the aim is to love. Those who do not love, those who do not know, are themselves a product of this hoax. . . .

December 13*th* 1859

You letters disturb me terribly, Princess; your ideas and your dreams immediately set my mind afire. If I had been twenty years younger you would be able to make something of me. But what can one expect? I need quiet, peace of mind and health to achieve whatever it may be. And if, moreover, you knew how I waste my time—I hardly make good use of more than one hour out of forty. What plans can I make with such habits, with a life thus torn to pieces? Out of these forty hours, twenty at least are spent in suffering one way or another, twelve at least in sleep and seven in trying to make ends meet by the absurd things one has to do in order to live. Recently, on a visit to Madame Viardot, where there was a musical party, the harmonies I heard gave me a sudden shock and I seemed to see, surrounded by a strange halo, our Cleopatra. Yes, indeed, I think I could make a seductive creature of this fish; it would be completely different from anything I have so far done. And there would be such a chance for the strange and the unusual. I fancy I should merely borrow certain details from Shakespeare and would then do my best to give my fantasy a free rein. I should first require the setting of an interior of a Pyramid, and then the Priests of Isis, with their mysterious rites and impostures. Something more exaggerated will be required to portray Cleopatra. Then there will be the scene of Cydnus. I must have a secret orgy of the women with the eunuch Mardian as a counterpart to the public orgy of the triumvirs on the slave-ships of the young Pompey. There might also be a way of bringing together the cold, calculating Octavia with the crazy

Egyptian herself. What a contrast! Yes, it would be interesting. But time is necessary, time and life. I consider myself happy enough to have finished and corrected over this last year my score of *Les Troyens*. I am aware of the value of the grace that has been granted me. The proverb speaks well: "Grasp all, lose all".

It is of course painfully discouraging to imagine the likely fate of these great musical conceptions. Wherever you look you see great donkeys and little puppies, not to speak of the swine who poke their snouts in the artist's domains. What is the point of cultivating exotic fruits, sugar canes and palm-trees?

Great God, how sad is life! Forgive me, Princess; it seems that I have become now one of the idols of Gomorrha and that my eyes are to be filled with tears of lava. Away with the outside world! The feelings are there but one cannot express them; or one expresses them but they are not understood. One conceives on an immense scale but actually produces something petty. One craves for the free air and one merely buries one-self; instead of taking flight with the wings of an eagle one crawls like a worm. Aspirations belong to another world, but our needs are animal needs. Thunder may be in the heart, but actions in life go for nothing.

You see that I am taking the permission you gave me, to think aloud with you, at your word. Your mind and soul are filled with so much kindness; do not mock me, do not believe I am crazy and bombastic. All this may only be my sickness. To whom may I lament in this way if not to you. . . .

TO MADAME ESTELLE FORNIER
March 4th 1867

I must ask you to forgive me for the last letter which I took the liberty of sending you. I was so ill that I hardly knew what I was writing. But you will have been good and kind enough to forgive me.

Now although I am still suffering greatly, my mind is somewhat freer. I have just returned from Cologne where I was engaged to conduct two of my scores on Febraury 26th. I twice refused the offer; the third time I agreed and without really knowing what this journey would yield I decided to go. I had some extremely bad attacks, it is true; but I was all the same able to direct three rehearsals and the concert in the evening. The Capellmeister, Herr Hiller, an old friend of mine whose true feelings I had misunderstood, turned out to be most friendly. We made up our old differences. His orchestra was admirable and the response of the public most warm. My scene from *Béatrice et Bénédict* and my big symphony *Harold en Italie* were splendidly performed. As in Vienna I was offered a magnificent supper: fanfares, speeches and so on.

Back here I am resting completely, and with this I have a positive loathing of music, a horror of listening to it, also a feeling of sadness at not seeing you, the fear of vexing you, a return of my physical pains, troubles of all kinds and a sense of the heaviness of life. Whatever your philosophical outlook I fear that you too must be suffering in this way. I imagine that you are not spared concern either in your wintry solitude, among the great bare trees in that far-off estate of yours and the monotonous life to which you have chosen to resign yourself—and the ennui, the ennui. If only I were wrong!

If I were as I used to be I should write you of things which you might find pleasant and even amusing. Alas, such letters would be very forced from me nowadays and you would surely find them pitiful. I have no longer anything mischievous to boast of and I am now incapable of describing the amusing things of life to which in any case I fancy you are indifferent. Surrounded by your charming family you are fortunately immune to stupid and evil-minded people.

My hope however is that you will not remain unaffected by the sudden impulses of my poor heart which persists in showing some life instead of slowly fading away.

If only I had forgotten you! No, no—I see, as if it were yesterday, Meylan and your romantic home, and yourself in this setting young and sublimely beautiful—and I recall too my own wretched youth.

Forgive me: my tears cannot be restrained; I had better stop. Let my lips respectfully touch your hand and ask your pardon for my ramblings.

Hector Berlioz

GEORGES BIZET
[1838-1875]
EDOUARD LALO
[1823-1892]
CAMILLE SAINT-SAËNS
[1835-1921]

*T*he letters of Bizet display a curious jumble of observations. The sharp eye of the composer of Carmen wanders over the surface of the Italian landscape and selects also, in these letters, the animated street scenes of Rome and Paris. These vivid scenes are not recorded without a suggestion of lust, but Bizet's wandering eye does not probe. In Rome he joins in the Carnival. What would one not give to see re-enacted the description the young Bizet gives of himself, heavily moustached, dressed up in the prettiest of baby's clothes and showering flowers on the prettiest of the Roman girls? He tells his mother, too, of some frightful goings-on in Italy: "There is not one woman here in a hundred who has not a Cardinal, a Bishop or a Priest." Already we may glimpse during Bizet's student days in Rome the streak of sensuality that was soon to become ingrained in his music.

The intensity of his passionate nature was sometimes uncontrollable: in Venice, overcome with grief on learning of the illness of his mother he "picks a quarrel with a gondolier with the one idea of strangling him." Later as a soldier in the Garde Nationale during the uprisings of the Paris Commune, the imaginative master of the dramatic stage sets down in harrowing detail the disasters caused by "gangs of fire-brands, brigands and cannibals".

He is appalled by "bad nineteenth-century Italian taste". But some of his judgements, seen from this distance of time, seem to us very quaint indeed. He deplores the fact that (in 1858) the Italians know nothing of a curious succession of composers, "Rossini, Mozart,

Weber, Paer and Cimarosa". He then proceeds to put Mozart and Rossini on the same level ("the two greatest musicians"), and these he contrasts with Beethoven and Meyerbeer to whom "everything in me responds". Equally surprising is Bizet's judgement on the middle-period Verdi, a man of genius, he admits, but who lacks "style" and "who is following the most deplorable direction".

It is interesting to see in the letters of the more mature Bizet a sign of a malady that was later to become common enough—the self-consciousness of style. "To imitate is idiotic. Rather produce a poor imitation of oneself than of someone else." Here an adolescent trait persists rather unexpectedly in a composer of Bizet's stature. Fifty years later another stylist, Ravel, takes the opposite stand: "I cannot pretend to compose out of the void; I can only hope to find something new by imitating." It looks as if style was the tyrannical mistress of Bizet's life. Once he had given everything to it in Carmen *it was the end.*

The letters of Edouard Lalo are included as a curiosity. Here, set out at length, is the notorious French mistrust of Brahms. Beethoven, Schumann, Schubert, Mendelssohn—to French musical minds this was approximately the hierarchy of the beloved German Romantics. But Brahms—never! The idea of associating Brahms's wealth of warm melody with the lyrical spontaneity of Schumann was monstrous. *Lalo spoke for a whole generation in consistently denying to Brahms not only a sense of the orchestra—this is understandable—but anything beyond an academic gift of melody. Even accounting for Brahms's staid severity, which might have repelled the more nimble French minds, the lack of response throughout this period to Brahms remains incomprehensible. Even far into the twentieth century the barrier is still there.* Quoi! *exclaimed Ravel, derisively whistling to a visiting conductor the opening of the Passacaglia of the Brahms Fourth. "Vous n'allez pas jouer cette valse-là à Paris?"*

The abuse poured on the great Violin Concerto by Lalo and his Spanish friend Sarasate should be read, however, with the knowledge that Lalo's Rhapsodie Espagnole *was the musical equivalent of a Manet; the gulf between Latins and Teutons was wide. Also in justice* to the general picture of the period there does seem to have been an underground Parisian movement in support of Brahms. These supporters, Les Brahmines, led by Edouard Schuré and Hugues Imbert, succeeded in nominating Brahms as a member of the French Academy and raising contributions from Fauré, Chausson, d'Indy and some fifty other musical figures for the cost of the Brahms monument in Vienna.

A strain of gentle irony runs through the essays, and also some of the amateur rhymes, of the largely forgotten Saint-Saëns. As a critic Saint-Saëns was narrow and hedged around with personal prejudices. Although he lived on until 1921, alone his protégé Fauré was the composer he admired of a later generation. His detractors maintain that what he provided was nothing more than de la mauvaise musique bien écrite. A life-long enemy of Debussy, he persisted in representing the crumbling conservative pillar in the music of his time. But there was an urbane humour in his view of things that is not unattractive. In England he discovers that the unmusicality of the English is a myth, he proclaims the glories of the Midland Choirs, but finds the unadventurousness of Birmingham audiences too conservative even for him: the Messiah had been established in the repertory for all time; now the Elijah is added, and one shudders to think, he says, what would happen if Birmingham were to add a third such work to be played for all eternity. In Cambridge the composer of the Carnival des Animaux is greatly amused at his investiture on the occasion of an honorary doctorate. In the company of his fellow doctor, Tchaikovsky and, following closely behind, the Maharajah of Bhaonagar decked out in fabulous jewels, he is made to parade the streets in his wonderful robes and to listen to a long, florid harangue addressed to him in Latin. A charming account is given of this picturesque English adventure which may send us back to his music in the hope of finding somewhere among it a little of the same mellowness and subtlety.

BIZET

Dear Mother,

   . . . I see that you have no idea of life at the French Academy here. You wonder whether I am interested in politics. Good Lord! No one knows what is happening nor do we want to know. We are artists and this means that anything not concerned with art and our personal welfare has no place in our lives at all. You are quite right: I had a wonderful time at the Carnival. We drove about in a carriage with some friends and threw handfuls of flowers and confetti all over the place. The Carnival at Rome is as lovely as can be. Pretty women at every window, mostly dressed in the typical Roman fashion. You are either smothered in flowers or whitewashed by the plaster confetti. If you happen to be in grey overalls you can throw flowers at the women or plaster confetti at the men, it won't change the colour. M. Schnéty gave a masked ball. The wife of one of our servants made a delightful baby's dress for me to wear. It was a huge success. . . . I am keeping all these souvenirs of the carnival to show you on my return, and to dress up in if you wish. . . .

   I've seen a little of Rome. There are many beautiful things but also many disappointing things. Italy is poisoned by bad taste. In the world of art it is past praying for. Rossini, Mozart, Weber, Paer, Cimarosa are unknown, despised or forgotten. A sad state of affairs! The Theatres are not open during the carnival; but there will be some imposing religious celebrations in Holy Week.

Rome, June 13th 1858

Dear Mother,

   . . . I have been on a wonderful journey. What a glorious

country! We have seen many, many things. You get to know more about the language and character of the Italian people in a fortnight with them in the mountains than in six months in Rome. Of course we were lucky. We have seen some of the most amusing and interesting things imaginable. At one place there was a wedding and a burial and elsewhere a very unusual procession. Everywhere the people were good and kindly. The Italian peasants have no dislike for the French and anyhow they are very easily pleased. For a cigar or two they will be on your side. The women are often pretty, sometimes ugly and always dirty. We visited several monasteries and everywhere we received a friendly welcome. Once we were received by a charming gentleman, a distinguished personality and most handsome in appearance. The kindly but serious look on his face was indeed inspiring. He wore his monk's robes with a wonderful naturalness and elegance. Half of the towns we have visited are stricken with disease, all the houses of the Pontine Marshes are infected with malaria and there is a feverish look on every face. It hasn't been too hot. In Italy when the sun isn't shining it isn't stuffy. In fact when the sun sets it is cold, very cold. I have many more things to tell you about my journey but I'll keep them for my next letter.

June 25th 1858

Dear Mother,

. . . I have only time to tell you that what impressed me most was the innocence of the natives. By "innocence" I mean "ignorance", for there are no chaste women here above the price of one franc and most of the men will do anything asked of them for a few sous. The same applies to the upper classes except that it is more expensive. There is not one woman here in a hundred who has not a Cardinal, a Bishop or a Priest, according to her standing.

I am full of admiration for the virtuous Italian women. I put them on a higher level than Joan of Arc or Lucretia. I was hoping when I left Paris that I should be rid of light-hearted women but I've been frankly unlucky. I am sure you must be tremendously angry, but what can I do? You, the rare virtuous women of this world, inspired by the love of your families, you apparently do not realise that you deserve a thousand times more than the Holy Martyrs. You may not believe it; but we do.

Rome, October 8th 1858

Dear Mother,

. . . I want to speak about myself and the music I am writing. I am very busy just now for I believe that my little opera [*Don Procopio*] might well develop into an excellent work, and the more I become convinced of this the more I am determined to persevere. I want it to hold together as a uniformly good work without any weak patches. This is of course the difficulty. I have fortunately changed in regard to such matters: I can now go over my work, and to advantage. You remember that when I wrote something in Paris I could never go over it and improve upon it. Here I find that I am delighted to do so. And here's another sign of development: I feel that all my musical skill and application are of no further use to me; I can write nothing without an inspiring idea, so that there will be nothing in my opera devoid of interest. I am convinced that it is better to do something bad than something mediocre—and what I am trying to do is something good which will be better still. I have terrific difficulty in composing, which is only natural: I have nothing to compare my work with, and I can only be happy with what I've done when I know it to be *good*— whereas at the Conservatoire I was content merely to write something better than the music of my class-mates.

So you see I am taking these matters seriously. I am aware too of the development of my artistic allegiances. The contacts between painters, sculptors and musicians are a contributory cause. All the arts are inter-connected, or rather all art is one, regardless of whether an artist's vision is projected on to a canvas, in marble or on the stage. I am more than ever convinced that Mozart and Rossini are the two greatest musicians. Whilst everything in me responds to Beethoven and Meyerbeer, by my nature I am more interested in the ease of abstract art than in dramatic passion. Raphael was the same kind of person as Mozart; Meyerbeer felt as Michelangelo felt. Don't think that I am becoming self-opinionated. Not at all: I am coming round to the belief that Verdi is a man of genius who is following the most deplorable directions imaginable.

Here, then, are a few rough ideas on my artistic development since I left. I am pleased to say that my personal outlook has not changed. I am constantly alive though more serious-minded. It is a fact that everyone believes that there will be no obstacles in my path and that I shall go straight ahead. I wish it were so, but I am fearful of the way back, of meeting theatre managers and librettists whom I shall not grace with the name of poets. I am fearful of the singers, and in a word of all that unspoken criticism which is never expressed in unpleasant terms but which does nevertheless hold an artist back. . . .

You perhaps find me naive in paying myself all these compliments. But I am telling you the truth so that you should know how far I have got and so that you should have a quiet mind about me. I embrace you both with all my heart and assure you that I am the most loving of sons.

February 19th 1859

Dear Mother,

. . . We have already had twenty discussions [with Felicien David] on the subject of Verdi. This is my opinion—different from the opinion I held in Paris but here I am able to judge dispassionately: Verdi is a man of great talent without that quality of the great masters, namely style. But there are wonderful flights of passionate feeling in his music. It is fierce brutal passion, it is true, but it is better thus than that there should be no passion at all. His music is sometimes exasperating but never dull. Really I fail to understand either the enthusiasm or the criticism that he has aroused. His music doesn't warrant all this. . . .

Venice, September 5th 1860

Dear Mother,

I have been in Venice two hours. It was very unwise of you to send me a letter from a nursing home. This was the first letter handed to me by the postman and which I immediately tore open. The blow was frightful! I began reading the first two lines, blood rushed to my eyes and I simply couldn't go on. Then, after a quarter of an hour's agony, I decided to pick a quarrel with a gondolier and threw myself at him with the one idea of strangling him. It was our good friend Guiraud who tore us apart. Two minutes later I landed at the Piazza S. Marco. The sight of these wonderful scenes brought me back to my senses and I decided to leave for Paris. Here again Guiraud came to my aid. "Read the letter first," he said; and indeed as I read it through I did find reason for a more balanced view of things. . . .

TO EDMOND GALABERT

October 1866

. . . I believe that our entire future is connected with the perfection of a social policy. In society perfected there will be no more injustice and thus no malcontents and no attempt to sabotage the social bargain; no more priests, policemen or crime, no more adultery or prostitution, no more live emotion or passion—but wait a minute!—no more music, no more poetry, no *Légion d'honneur*, no Press (good riddance to that!), no theatres, no imprudence and therefore no more art. Confound it all! Where have you led me? Your inevitable unrelenting progress spells the death of art. You don't believe a word of what I am saying, I'm sure. Art originated in societies

Saint-Saëns [1913]

Lalo [c. 1890]

Saint-Saëns [c. 1871]
Caricature by Gabriel Fauré

georges Bizet
revenant de l'école Française de Rome
en Septembre 1860;
(croquis fait en wagon de Chambéry à Combières
par gaston Planté)

Bizet [1860]
Drawing by
Gaston Planté

Ernest van Dyck
and Chabrier
[1890]

infected with superstition: Egypt had its architecture, Greece the plastic arts, the Renaissance Raphael, and Mozart, Beethoven, Veronese and Weber were half mad! The Fantastic, Hell, Paradise, the Jinns, phantoms, ghosts, fairies—there is the domain of art! Try and prove to me that there could be any art based on reason, truth and fact. . . . As a musician, I declare that if you suppress adultery, fanaticism, crime, imprudence and the supernatural it would be impossible to write another note. I'd even go so far as to say that I'd write better music if I believed everything that is untrue. . . .

TO HIPPOLYTE RODRIGUES

Paris, March 20th 1871[1]

. . . If you want to know the truth here it is: thirty thousand men in Montmartre, Bellevue and other such neighbourhoods, of which twenty-five thousand had decided to take flight at the first outburst of firing. A committee was formed but was extremely embarrassed by what had gone on and its one idea was to have no responsibility for it.

30,000 men in Paris—this was the most shameful state of affairs! 30,000 cowards and scoundrels they are, ever so much worse than those crazy people in control. It's disgraceful. When I say 30,000 cowards I should say 25,000, for about 5000 men (and I was one of them [in a battalion of the Garde Nationale]) offered themselves to the government. Although we were only a handful, inadequately armed, we would have marched. We hung about for eighteen hours without seeing a superior officer or receiving an order. . . . At midnight some kind of staff officer came along and advised us to go home.

The whole of Paris was on the streets smoking cigars and asking what the news was. Those in command hardly dared to show their noses. No my friend, Paris will never overcome this shame. It would be absolutely laughable if it weren't the

---

[1] The uprising of the Commune took place in Paris on March 18th.

D

certain sign of the death of a whole society. And what the *Journal officiel* says about pillaging is a pack of lies. Not a pin was stolen. . . . Yesterday, a lovely day, the town was on holiday. I swear I am not exaggerating a thing.

. . . . I knew what this insurrection would amount to, but I believed that Paris still had a few drops of blood in her veins. I was very sadly mistaken. . . .

Well don't worry, there's no danger for us. Paris has taken too long to become a blood-bath. There are no more revolutions nowadays, only parodies of revolutions. Crime has become something quite exceptional. . . .

TO MADAME HALÉVY

May 27th 1871[1]

We spend our time on the rooftops, on high embankments, hillsides, lamp-posts and other such elevated positions. We go about with a map to discover where we are and in the hope of finding some of our wretched belongings. . . . The newspapers which have exaggerated the extent of the frightful disasters have mentioned no fires in our neighbourhood. The gangs of firebrands, brigands and cannibals which have fallen on Paris and to whom I hope sensible people will attribute no political motives, have been deprived of their ring-leaders. I was speaking yesterday to an officer who had returned from Paris. He was very impressed: the soldiers are furious and have taken to shooting at random. . . . Passy had a frightful time. Yesterday everything seemed to be over when at nine o'clock we saw a gigantic fire over Paris—they say it may be the Magasins Réunis. Paris will certainly get rid of these queer men and especially these queer women who have provoked these awful riots—and we shall at last be able to breathe freely again. I shall go to Paris as soon as possible. But any kind of movement in or out of the town is still strictly forbidden.

[1] The army of Marshal MacMahon entered Paris on May 24th.

TO MADAME HALÉVY

May 29th 1871

. . . The crimes committed are frightful enough. . . . To break up this vast international association of rogues is our first duty. The second is not to be influenced by the Catholic reaction. Let us hope for the best. . . .

As for ourselves, we really had nothing to fear since we were *protected*(!) by a German garrison. . . .

I shan't speak to you of Wagner today. . . . It is the fate of genius to be misunderstood by contemporary society. Wagner is not exactly a friend of mine, and I have only a moderate opinion of him. But I shall never forget the immense joys which this original genius has given me. The appeal of his music with all its undertones of voluptuousness and love is indescribable.

If I were to play you his music for a week you would go mad about it. The Germans, who I'm afraid are, musically, certainly superior to us, realise that Wagner is one of their greatest productions. He incarnates the whole of German 19th century thought. . . .

I don't go so far as to put Wagner on the level of Beethoven, as you do. Beethoven is not a man: he is a god, like Shakespeare, Homer and Michelangelo. And what do we find? Consider the fact that the most enlightened public listens every year to the greatest example of music, namely the Choral Symphony, without understanding a single thing. . . .

Of course if I set out to imitate Wagner I shouldn't write another note in my life, despite my admiration for him. To imitate is idiotic. Rather produce a poor imitation of oneself than of someone else. And in fact the more wonderful the model, the more pitiful the imitation. Michelangelo, Shakespeare and Beethoven have been imitated, and with what appalling results we know. . . .

LALO

TO PABLO DE SARASATE

August 28th 1878

Dear friend,

I write to you today in a state of incredible amazement. It is the Second Symphony in D of Brahms that has brought me to this state. I read it yesterday morning and heard it later in the day at the Concert Populaire. So this is the fellow that some people place above and others on a level with Schumann! Schumann, the great poet, the mighty inspired musician every note of whom is *his own*, and the composer of the Second D major Symphony on the same level: it's sheer craziness!

Brahms is an inferior mind who has investigated every peculiarity of modern counterpoint and harmony. This is his only quality: he is not a born musician. His imagination is invariably insignificant or it is merely a pastiche: the pastiche in his latest symphony is particularly glaring.[1] I know all his chamber music very well; it holds it own because it has a thorough technical grounding, but its imagination is feeble and you are aware of a man anxious to find whatever he can grasp to mask the void in himself. Moreover, from a desire to build up sonority for its own sake there is a tremendous abuse of unison writing. (Beethoven knew enough about harmony to realise the value of unisons, but he was able to achieve sonorous effects without resorting to them). Then came the Piano Quintet. Something burst out of this work which made us think that the composer had at last found himself. But alas! the following works, all remarkable for their technical skill, are absolutely insignificant in regard to musical imagination. Since these last chamber works I had seen nothing of this

---

[1] Lalo is referring, of course, to the C minor Symphony.

46

composer and before yesterday's concert I had never heard an
orchestral work of his. You will perhaps say that Pasdeloup's
performance was inadequate. It may be, but that would apply
to all other works, and in any case Pasdeloup had carefully
rehearsed this new symphony which is not difficult. In fact at
this very concert they played a Symphony in G of Mozart
which is a dwarf by the side of an orchestral work of Beethoven but which, compared to the Symphony of Brahms, was
a Colossus. The first and the last movements are thin and old-
fashioned in ideas, and all the themes of his developments
derive constantly from Mendelssohn and Beethoven. The
Andante offers a contrast to these puerile movements but is no
less dull. It produces the effect of someone acting the part of an
heroic character and pronouncing such bombastic platitudes as:
"With this sword I proclaim a new life!" or "The State Chariot
is rocked by a volcano!" The Scherzo is a pretty little stylised
piece.

But what is really unbelievable is the orchestration of
Brahms. He has no idea of the differentiation of timbres, he
orchestrates like a pianist, and if one of us had produced some
such second-rate example of orchestral skill we should very
soon send him back to the class-room.

It comes down to the fact that the Quintet, which I believed
was going to open up a new world to be explored by this
sturdy figure now in full possession of his powers, turns out
to represent the climax of his career, for he has since continuously declined, and his latest symphony is worth less than the
least of his quartets.

Something quite ridiculous occurred at this concert. The
work was hissed—by the very same people who had just
encored an absurd re-hash of Taubert. Whereupon I applauded
extravagantly, for the simple reason that extremes must be
met by extremes and that it is in my opinion appalling that
such fools should hiss an artist whose stature I may question
but whose standing is not to be challenged. As for his

symphony it is, as I say, a work that should be neither applauded nor hissed.

I met Saint-Saëns at the concert; his opinion of the symphony is the same as mine. This is indeed a long letter but I wanted to show you what the reputation of Brahms beyond the Rhine amounts to: the mountain has given birth to a mouse.

TO PABLO DE SARASATE

September 21st 1878

What you tell me of the respect which attaches to the name of Brahms in Germany doesn't surprise me: the Germans treat everything that belongs to them as a fetish and they extol their favourite figures in such an exaggerated way that they have managed to make everyone else think that those of us who do not think as they do are mere fools. We in France are at fault in achieving just the contrary. Of the two I prefer the German attitude but this is not a reason to pocket any sort of affront, for that is what this question of the genius of Brahms is. The word genius presupposes something of the poetry and the imagination of Schumann or Schubert. Brahms has none of this. Take any of the late quartets of Beethoven and you are immediately aware of what genius means; take the whole of the work of Brahms and you see a man of talent and nothing more. In his Second Symphony there are flagrant thefts from Schubert and Mendelssohn, and since he was bent on taking the latter as a model he might well have imitated his luminous orchestration, for his texture would not then have been so doughy. The form of this Symphony is old-fashioned, his imagination meagre and his orchestration is that of a pupil who appears not to know whether to use a clarinet or an oboe. If they were not such idol-worshippers the sensible German musicians would realise as much. They are sufficiently rich in tremendous musical glories not to proclaim as a genius a musician of talent whose stature doesn't reach the ankles of their giants.

I had a real set-to on this subject with the Szarvadys. "You
don't understand it," she said to me in her markedly superior
way. "You must hear this masterpiese many times." As it
happens Madame Szarvady had herself heard this masterpiece
only once, but her great mind was able to appreciate every
note. The fact is that Brahms is a creation of Madame Szarvady
and no one must say a thing against him. She is an idol-
worshipper of the first water. Driven to exasperation, I took it
upon myself to demolish her idol, as I am normally inclined to
do in such cases, with the result of course that I was put down as
nothing but a poor wretch of a musician incapable of approaching such sublime regions.

TO PABLO DE SARASATE

August 27th 1879

Yesterday at the Châtelet Madame Szarvady won the day:
she played well and each movement of the Concerto [the First
Concerto by Brahms] was greatly applauded. After the last
movement there was some hissing which was obviously intended for the work. It turned out that this absurd demonstra-
tion served Madame Szarvady very well for the entire hall
began to shout "Out with them!" and the applause redoubled.
This was the fifth time I had heard this Concerto and my feeling
about it is the same: it is all very interesting and the first movement is very fine. But I believe that when you have a soloist
on the platform he should be brought into prominence and
not dealt with as if he were a member of the orchestra. If a
composer is not attracted by such solo work, let him write
symphonies or anything he likes for the orchestra, but don't
let us have little solo bits constantly interrupted by the orchestra
and which are moreover much less interesting than what the
orchestra has just played. The Brahms Concerto is a large-scale
orchestral work and when the piano comes in with its inter-
ludes I find it annoying. The Concertos of Beethoven and
Mendelssohn are symphonically conceived in the same way as

the Brahms Concerto, but I am interested in the soloist in the former whereas in the latter I feel uneasy about him. . . . On this occasion the French public, so often discredited, deserves a good mark for the work is long and uniform in mood, and they listened to it attentively and gave the interpreter her due.

TO PABLO DE SARASATE

November 8th [1879]

I have just been reading the violin concerto of Brahms. I can understand that such a work might be written when one happens not to have any sort of idea in one's mind; but I fail to understand how it can be allowed to go out into the world when the composer looks it over some months after his failure.

The Piano Concerto is a beautiful score, whatever one might say about the role of the soloist by comparison with the concertos of Beethoven and Schumann. But in the Violin Concerto the inspiration is meagre, and despite all the composer's efforts to increase his effects by means of all the tricks of the trade, he is unable to mask the poverty of his musical thought. [The D major theme of the first movement; Lalo writes out this theme] might go down well played by a horn in some valley in Switzerland, with a *la-la-i-tou* at the end. [The oboe theme of the Adagio] might rival the Berceuse of Reber; [and the opening theme of the last movement] would make a good effect in the collections of Studies by Dancla. With these three commonplace ideas, the only cantabile themes in the work, Brahms constructs his Concerto. The remainder consists of orchestral developments on these three vulgar themes, and over these the violin repeats from one end of the work to the other the dullest and the most sloppy figures that I have ever seen written for this instrument. I fear that the fate of Brahms will be the same as the fate of—you know whom I mean. His fanatical admirers go into raptures when he does the most commonplace things and it seems to me that in his recent works God seems to have abandoned him.[1]

[1] Sarasate's opinion of the Brahms Concerto seems to have corresponded exactly to that of his friend. In reply to A. Moser's question as to whether he was going to include it in his repertory, he is reported to have replied: "Do you think that I am so deprived of taste as to stand on the platform like a listener, holding my violin in my hand while the oboe plays the only melody in the whole work?" (Quoted in *Musiciens peints par eux-mêmes*, by Marc Pincherle, Paris, 1939, p. 182).

SAINT-SAËNS

IT is worth dwelling on the large scale of the Birmingham musical festivals, their long tradition and their value to English people. As in the Rhineland, a Festival at Birmingham consists of a number of concerts spread over several days. We have nothing like this in France where we pretentiously call a "Festival" any kind of concert that is out of the ordinary. Alone the musical celebrations in the west of France have something of the character of the English and German festivals; but even these are much less ambitious schemes.

Strange as it may seem, the musical life of England is still very little known on the continent and one is astonished at the strange ideas current in Paris on the musical outlook of our neighbours. Simply because some compatriot of Shakespeare has been heard to sing in a drawing-room with a cracked voice, the conclusion has been arrived at that the English are anti-musical. They are said to be indiscriminate in their welcome to musicians and to be influenced only by publicity and celebrity. Many a visiting musician to England has discovered to his cost that the truth is nothing of the sort. Of course, when an artist does not receive the success abroad that he had expected, he is not inclined to proclaim as much to all and sundry at home. Thus the French public has sometimes been under the impression that Madame X or Mlle Y have had London at their feet when in fact nothing of the kind has occurred. I could if I wish open a Pandora's box on this subject. But fear not; I shall keep these secrets to myself. . . .

The great quality of the English public is that they are patient. They are reserved but not by nature suspicious nor excessively

enthusiastic. Yet they are not grudging. Extremely conservative, they appear never to tire of certain time-honoured
works however hackneyed they may be. On the other hand,
they are ready to listen to new and even revolutionary works
and are as eager as anyone to come to terms with them. If a
new work fails to make an impression, they merely refrain from
applause but without making a show of open hostility. In a
word they are relaxed. Which means too that they are not
given to modern thrills, to those wild outbursts of packed
audiences in other countries on which an artist with his natural
love of danger is apt to thrive. Have they their limitations?
One cannot anywhere expect the ideal. . . .

I should like all those people who have been talking about the
unmusicality of the English to hear the Birmingham choir.
They have everything: intonation, rhythm, a careful shading
of dynamics and a lovely sound. If these people are not musicians then, I say, they certainly act as if they were the best
musicians in the world. You may, for instance, ask them at a
moment's notice to change any matter of expression or tempo
and you will find that they will immediately respond to your
wishes. Passages of difficult intonation and dangerous pianis-
simos in the high register are child's play to them. It is incon-
ceivable that such singers have not in them the true spirit of
music. But even if this did turn out to be true, the credit due
to them would be even greater, for other supposedly more
musical choirs have not so far reached this level. Let us then
frankly acknowledge such superior qualities in others. . . .

In England the oratorio style springs from Handel, and it is
his works that are the daily bread of all musical celebrations.
Ever since the inauguration of the Birmingham Festival there
has not been a single Festival year without the *Messiah*. And
now that Mendelssohn's *Elijah* has scored a triumph at Birmingham, this too is never omitted. These two works are thus
destined to be played for all time at each of the Birmingham
Festival's programmes. There is obviously a certain dullness in

this scheme of things and indeed one shudders at the thought of a third work finding such favour with the Birmingham public.

This apparent narrowness of outlook is by no means a purely musical matter. The English love of the oratorio has a religious basis which in origin is very strange. England has been a Catholic country and a Protestant country. But at heart England is neither Protestant like the Germanic peoples, nor Catholic like the Latin races. England is a Biblical country and the standing of the Old Testament in English religious life is almost the standing it has with the Jews. Hence the appeal of works such as *Israel in Egypt*, *Elijah* and *Solomon*, the subjects of which would never mean as much in other countries as in England. All the same the work which everywhere in England still enjoys the greatest success is the *Messiah*. The fact is that in English eyes the Gospel itself belongs to this Biblical tradition—a matter of which the foreign traveller in England is keenly aware and which is peculiarly difficult to convey to other peoples.

VISIT TO CAMBRIDGE

From time to time the University of Cambridge confers on various people the degree of Doctor *honoris causa*. The government in England is in no way concerned with these awards, contrary to the opinion of certain people who see the government connected in one way or another with every aspect of public life. Cambridge confers doctorates in the faculties of Law, Letters, Science and Music. . . . Five Doctors of Music were created on this occasion, Max Bruch, Peter Tchaikovsky, Arrigo Boito, Edvard Grieg and the author of these lines. This abundance of musicians was due to the fact that the fiftieth anniversary was to be celebrated that year of the Cambridge University Musical Society. The English, as we all agree, are not a musical people, whereas we are musicians to our finger-tips. Yet I do not know that any of our University faculties of

Letters or Sciences has taken under its wing a Musical Society
with a flourishing chorus and orchestra able to give in its own
hall concerts of old and modern music of all schools. . . .

Better qualified writers than I have described the English
universities and I shall be content merely to speak of my
pleasure in visiting the delightful town of Cambridge with its
groups of Gothic buildings set amongst the green fields. Each
college is provided with a Chapel—if this name may be used
for what is properly a Cathedral—and there the surpliced
students daily attend service, singing in chorus. This religious
aspect of English university life strikes us as most odd and one
cannot think that the ordinary French student would be very
happy under such conditions. Yet the demands made in the
name of religion in England are relatively few. The service,
which is very short, consists principally of listening to some
splendid music very well sung, for the English have excellent
choirs. I heard in one of the Colleges a choral work by Barnby,
very fine in feeling, faultless in technique, not unlike the
choral writing of Gounod or Mendelssohn. The Anglican
church is a serious and artistic shrine, not at all a frightening
place of worship such as our Catholic church where the real
presence and the confession provoke terror. The transition
from the English home, with its strict decorum, to the place
of worship is hardly noticeable, as indeed is the transition from
the typical gentleman to the married clergyman, a family
man enjoying society as much as anyone. There may be a little
more severity of outlook in one field than in the other, but
nothing more. . . .

All those who know me are aware how reluctant I am to
receive honours and to take part in official meetings. Consequently I was somewhat apprehensive about going to Cambridge. . . . I was obliged, contrary to my normal practice,
to accept the hospitality, which I had first refused, of the
President of the Musical Society, the Provost of King's
College. "It is usual for our most distinguished guests to stay

at our homes," they wrote to me "and our committee would indeed be hard put to find an explanation for allowing the French representative to be satisfied with the hospitality of an hotel." I was of course unable to resist an invitation couched in such terms.

The ceremony, conceived principally as a tribute to music, was preceded by a concert given the day before, the programme of which was not exactly easy to put together. Five composers were to be represented, in fact six including Mr. Charles Stanford, the conductor of the Society, and this required some organisation. . . . The programme finally agreed upon ran as follows:—

1.	Fragment from *Ulysses* (Op. 41) ..	Max Bruch
2.	*Africa*, Fantasy for piano and orchestra	Saint-Saëns
3.	Prologue to *Mefistofele*	Boito
4.	Symphonic Poem, *Francesca da Rimini* (Op. 32)	Tchaikovsky
5.	Suite, *Peer Gynt* (Op. 45)	Grieg
6.	Ode, *East to West* (Op. 52)	Stanford

After the concert a banquet was held for a hundred people to celebrate the fiftieth anniversary of the Musical Society. The Doctors of Letters and Law were not among the guests. The place of honour, to the right of the President, was offered to me and I was told that I would be required to reply, on behalf of my colleagues, to Mr. Stanford's toast. This distinction was due not to my abilities but to my age. I am normally fearful of speaking in public but now I was required to put my best foot forward. Generally on such occasions all sorts of ideas pass through my mind which I daren't express. But on this occasion, in view of the very warm welcome, I did not restrain myself at all, *mêlant le grave au doux, le plaisant au sévère* in the manner peculiar to the many speeches that are made in England, and my fellow-doctors declared themselves very well pleased with what I had to say.

The following day was the investiture. It was in a fairly large hall with admission on invitation only. The students were seated in a circular gallery above. They began by dressing us up in large silk gowns with wide sleeves half white, half red, and providing us with head-dresses of mortar-boards in black torsade velvet with golden tassels. In this attire we set out on a procession through the town in the burning sun. At the head of the group of Doctors walked the King of Bhaonagar in a gold turban sparkling with fabulous jewels, and below his head a diamond necklace. I must confess that, normally hostile to the nondescript nature of our modern clothes, I was delighted with this parade.

Those taking part in the procession took their place on a dais and the ceremony proper began by speeches in prose and verse, in English and Latin. Now and again one of the students would interrupt with a quip; people would begin to laugh, the orator would politely wait until the laughter died down and go on with his speech. I remember the time when incidents of this sort occurred at the Institut de France at the prize distribution of the Académie des Beaux-Arts; they have however been stopped without anyone being the better off.

Now the speeches are over, an Assessor accompanied by a mace-bearer carrying a great silver mace calls upon each of the Doctors to rise, and after preaching to him in Latin presents him to the President, clothed in ermine, who acknowledges him as a Doctor *in nomine Patris, et Filii, et Spiritus Sancti*. He then shakes hands with him and thereupon the audience lets forth a tremendous burst of applause. The Latin speeches are in the most florid style. Homer and Schiller are referred to in the speech on Max Bruch, and Propertius in the speech on Tchaikovsky. Here, as a curiosity, is the speech pronounced in my honour:

> Yesterday, a certain society dedicated to the cultivation of the art of music among ourselves celebrated the completion of fifty prosperous years since its foundation under the best of auspices. There was present

that very leader and standard-bearer who has for so long, and so felicitously, performed, as it were, the part of Apollo Musagetes amid
the choir of the Muses. There were also present other illustrious Profes-
sors of our happy art, from among whom there are some, brought hither
from various nations, whom we are today decorating with our degrees.
But there is a man who stands over all the rest, both by his age and
his experience, a man from a neighbouring country, counted among
the great ones, who, endowed with a well-nigh incredible memory,
has clearly proved by his own example that the Muses were the daughters
of Mnemosyne. As an interpreter of sacred music, how learned! As
a critic of the art of music, how subtle! How many countries he has
travelled to! Into how many corners of the earth, and to what a
multitude of listeners has his fame gone out! Let us rejoice that he, who
once celebrated Prometheus, the giver of heavenly fire, has himself so
many times and felicitously sent forth the heavenly gifts of his musical
art among so many nations! Let us rejoice also that the most distinguished author of *Samson* has woven fresh flowers for his crown of
praise from the story of Phryne.[1]

The *dux et signifer* (leader and standard-bearer) in this
speech, compared to Apollo Musagetes, is Mr. Stanford, who
was long conductor of the Society's concerts and now occupies
a high position at the Royal College of Music in London.

After the ceremony a banquet at the home of the President,
Provost of Christ College, in the Doctors' honour—we are
still in our robes—and then a walk through the gardens to
visit "Milton's Tree". We are kindly informed that this tree,
a very old mulberry tree, has no connection with the cantor of
Paradise Lost. In the pleasant shade of these trees my more fortunate colleagues were able to relax and to be entertained by
charming ladies; but I was off to Trinity College Chapel for I
was most anxious to try out the excellent organ there. In the
evening I took leave of my hosts and returned to London delighted with my journey and my reception.

(*Portraits et Souvenirs*, Paris, 1908).

[1]Translation of this speech kindly made from the Latin by Mr. A. M. Cain.

Chabrier [*c.* 1887]
Drawing by Edouard Détaille

Debussy [*c.* 1900]
Photograph by Pierre Louÿs

EMMANUEL CHABRIER

[1841–1894]

To readers of biographies of musicians who are anxious to see the living features of the man reflected in his work, the numerous letters of Emmanuel Chabrier offer particular gratification. It so happens that the literary talents of Chabrier, long prized by admirers of this engaging composer, are not far below his original musical gifts. It has even been said, by Joseph Désaymard, the collector and editor of the main bulk of his correspondence, that this correspondence would warrant publication on its literary value alone, so sharply-defined is the composer's exuberant and loveable personality. And indeed, readers who are not primarily interested in the music of Chabrier—his vintage works are not more than a dozen or so in number—may be content to look no further; they will find here the essence of this thoroughly unaffected bon enfant.

What is nowadays conveyed by the high spirits of España, *the* Marche Joyeuse *and the* Valses Romantiques *is of course very much a period charm. So it is too with the composer's correspondence, which is an exact counterpart of these works. Here, in Chabrier's witty chatter, or in his amusing records of the ramblings of a Frenchman in Spain, are caught, as in a vignette, the most affecting delights of the Second Empire. He writes of the period known as* le temps des cheveux et des chevaux, *and he is therefore abundant in a supply of racey anecdotes. We see the jovial native of Auvergne off with his numerous country relatives in a carriage and pair to a village wedding, his astute ear missing nothing of the local gossip, pouncing on the village organ to improvise a parody of a wedding march, eating himself sick at the evening banquet and dancing till daybreak with the prettiest of the country wenches. In Spain, parading through the streets of Seville in the costume of a Toreador, he finds the Spanish*

E
59

women irresistible—he tells his publisher in these letters no more than this—and the entire sequence of Chabrier's Spanish letters forms a remarkable literary document the full flavour of which has not been exactly easy to render in English. Chabrier's comic vein, in the wide variety of scenes he so pointedly depicts, may be chiefly esteemed for its period value; but I am not so sure that we do not find an extension of this same comic vein in certain figures of the present day: Chabrier's biting humour is echoed, surely, in some of the earlier music of Francis Poulenc; and even more clearly in the endearing characteristics of Fernandel.

Chabrier may have defined only a limited musical world. But his letters reveal unsuspected affinities of this world with the contemporary world of painting. The wonderful detail in his accounts of excursions in the mountains around Mont-Dore could only have been set down by a writer with the eye of a painter. There were, in fact, three or four personalities in Chabrier. Each of them might have developed independently. As a youth, at Amsterdam, what seems most to have impressed the budding composer were the Ruysdaels, the Hobbemas and the Rembrandts. He was a life-long friend of Manet, who painted his portrait, and it is interesting to see how, in defining his musical ideal, he immediately seizes on a pictorial metaphor: "If the only colours I could use were grey pearl and canary yellow with their various shades—well, no, I should not find them enough, even though there may be as many as three hundred varieties of grey pearl. Let's have a little red, Good God!" The composer of the farm-yard songs, Les Cigales, Les Gros Dindons *and the* Villanelle des petits cochons roses *was also a collector of paintings which have since become renowned museum pieces. Some of them were either given to him or sold to him privately by his friends Manet and Renoir, but others were bought with the windfall of a legacy, or to mark some happy domestic event. Among the thirty-eight pictures of his collection sold after his death were ten Manets, including the* Bar aux Folies-Bergères *(for which he paid 5830 francs) now in the National Gallery; five pictures of Renoir, who also painted his portrait, and others of Cézanne, Monet and Sisley.*

These literary and pictorial associations of Chabrier were, however, never fertilised in his music in the way that similar literary and pictorial associations were fertilised in the music of Debussy. It was, however, Chabrier and not Debussy who was the personal friend of the Impressionist painters, and it would have been all the more fascinating, therefore, to have Chabrier's opinion of the young Impressionist composer whose early works he must surely have known. Unfortunately, Debussy is not once mentioned in Chabrier's correspondence—unless we may infer a reference when he deplores the music of, "a few young people among us who torment themselves in getting three jaded chords out of their system—the same ones all the time." *This* "sick music" *sends the extrovert Chabrier into a towering rage:* "There's no life in it, no tune in it, they're not worth a rap." (Ça ne vit pas, ça ne chante pas, ça ne pète pas.)

If it was not the young Debussy, who, then, was the God of this musical wit? It was Wagner, the "man of bronze" *before whom he is in abject admiration (though at a party given by Cosima he maliciously hides a large unpalatable cake in a drawer of the Master's boiled shirts). To his neighbour Vincent d'Indy during a Bayreuth performance of* Tristan, "Ten years," *he exclaimed, literally sobbing,* "Ten years I've been waiting for that A on the cellos!" *But except possibly in his last opera,* Gwendoline *he never became submerged under the Wagnerian tidal-wave. In Karlsruhe, Munich and Vienna, where he persistently went about in a country cotton bonnet and never for a moment concealed his Parisian toupet, he courts Hans Richter and Felix Mottl (*"In Paris when the name of Mottl is mentioned we all bow very low"*). This courting was pursued by Chabrier in the belief that his charming light opera* Le Roi malgré lui, *though not pretending to rank with the Wagnerian glories, nevertheless had a pertinent contribution to make of its own. It certainly had. And Mottl does in fact arrange for performances of both* Le Roi malgré lui *and* Gwendoline *at all the Wagnerian strongholds in Germany, and later himself orchestrated the* Bourrée Fantasque *and the* Valses Romantiques *in a manner entirely appropriate to Chabrier's intentions.*

Here is proof that the work of this minor master was not just a passing Parisian vogue; it made its mark during Chabrier's lifetime in the wider international sphere; and his original, racey verve brims over in his music still.

CHABRIER

TO HIS PARENTS

Rotterdam, 1865

AT LAST I've found a pen that writes! Good Lord—never a dull moment. Delightful time at The Hague but how often I thought of dear old Jaubert and his eye for painting. A museum about as big as a pocket handkerchief, but what wonders! The cows of Paul Potter, the Anatomy Lesson of Rembrandt, and there are van der Elsts, Ruysdaels, van Ostades and Hobbemas galore; and two glorious Van Dycks. . . . At Scheveningen where I've been twice the women are rather more covered up than they were last year. A bare back now and again, anything more than that very seldom; anyhow the sea is perpetually rough and all of a sudden a wave crashes in front of your eyes and you see nothing more. . . . Tomorrow I leave for Antwerp. . . . For the last six days I haven't touched a piano; I begin to get very itchy and start running my fingers over my hat, on the table in front of me, over my neighbour's back, on anything that happens to be about. At Amsterdam— shall I tell you?—I went with a gang of commercial travellers to some kind of one-eyed café. Nothing there but a piano. I flung myself at it, and those boors were simply flabbergasted. Of course I had to play them the *Carnaval de Venise*, *O mon Fernand* and other rubbish of this sort. Otherwise they would have thought me a hopeless ass. But at any rate I was playing. . . . Something or other happens every day, and sometimes every night, but nothing really comes my way and eventually I get home safely. At the hotel drawing-room at Scheveningen there is a silly old piano with a few not bad-looking women about reading, sewing or playing whist. When I come in I ask them to dance, we have a jolly time, I pass the hat round for the local fishermen's charity and they carry me round shoulder high. . . .

TO M. GUSTAVE DESJARDINS
Paris, 1879

Monsieur,

I have to deal with some important business which necessitates my going to Bordeaux. I shall be most grateful if you will allow me three days' leave for this journey.

The above lines are for my dossier. Now, as I have never lied, and this is perhaps why I have earned the esteem of my superiors, I must tell you, between ourselves, the real truth, and here it is: I am not going to Bordeaux at all. For almost ten years I have had a mad craving—and you can imagine the state of mind this brings one to—to see *Tristan and Isolde* by Richard Wagner. This masterpiece can only be seen in Germany, and it is being played next Sunday in Munich.

I couldn't resist any longer, and I decided today to get a pass to Avricourt which, alas! is our present frontier. I have it, and I shall cover the rest of my expenses by scribbling bits of articles for *Le Temps* and *Le Petit Journal*.

There is my crime, sir. I confess it to you but not to Pelletier [Chabrier's immediate superior] who must know nothing about it. I beg you to give me your administrative pardon for this escapade and to believe in my sincere devotion. Wednesday morning at the latest I shall be back at the office.

TO MM. ENOCH AND COSTALLAT
San Sebastian July, 1882(?)

Dear friends,

The family arrived yesterday without undue bother. Little by little we'll settle into the life here, and in a week's time we shall be real Spaniards. Anyhow San Sebastian has a cosmopolitan veneer and the local colour is distinctly toned down. Which is not to say that it is anything like the rue Rochechouart, and not a bit like any of the Paris suburbs. Who said that the Pyrenees were no longer here? Who is the silly ass? Where is he? I've got an enormous slice of them in front of my window. It's like a backdrop at a theatre. The peaceful Urumea winds its way gently under my eyes and joins, or rather glides into the sea right here just a couple of yards away. The women are pretty. The men are well built and the full-busted señoras on the beach don't seem to know how to fasten their dresses properly. I must go about with a needle and cotton; I love to make myself useful.

I'm paying a lot for the hire of a pretty poor piano and my idea is to let the local choirmaster hear the incomparable beauties of *The Ring* which of course I've got stuck away in my trunk. I shan't speak about *Tristan* which has become part of the clothes I wear. . . . What's happened to the final version of *Gwendoline*? It would be a dream for me to write quietly three acts of something or other here. Let me know what you think. If G. hasn't yet got the score of *L'Etoile* why don't you take it along to him yourself arm-in-arm with K.? Isn't that a good idea?

Our affectionate thoughts for these ladies and my cordial feelings for you, my good friends.

TO MM. ENOCH AND COSTALLAT
San Sebastian, August 1882

My dear friends,

Forgive me for not having replied earlier to your most charming missive of the other day, but the fleas of this country haven't given me a moment's peace. I've been after them for a whole week. I fancy you know nothing of the fleas of Guipuzcoa and so I'll tell you. You won't often have an opportunity of learning things like this. The Spanish flea is eminently patriotic and is not inclined to emigrate. After the Carlist troubles with which they were deeply concerned they perished, alas, in considerable numbers. They were routed. They had to gather themselves together again but you can't imagine— and here is a lesson for us to ponder—how swiftly, with what perfect understanding the survivors marched back home.

They have their national song, their *Marseillaise*, a 3/4 tune in F major which a French composer, one Berlioz, introduced in his *Damnation of Faust* as in fact he also introduced the national air of Racoczky. Since the province of Guipuzcoa is one of the coolest of the peninsula the flea finds it chilly and eagerly seeks undulating ground, sheltered spots, moist and sweaty. They have a weakness, which I appreciate, for the body of women. That's where they are really at home. Their favoured target is the plump woman, some big lump of a lass, those enormous areas encircled by a corset big enough for a bull fight, those immense behinds like long-range guns and of course the navel, the poor old forgotten navel, the funnel-shaped navel like a crater. They are generally rather rakish in character and I could tell you stories that would make even the covers of the Litolff Collection blush. If you are very good that'll be a treat for the future.

Thank you for the very precise information you give me about E. . . . I am awaiting impatiently the manuscript of *Gwendoline*. And please thank that splendid chap K. who has just sent me from G. a libretto in 3 acts written by a bear with a sore head. By the end of the week you will receive the music for this work and I count on your usual kindness to deliver it immediately to our best engravers. Sunday next, the 6th, while you are holding the watering-can in one hand and throwing kisses to your women-folk with the other, just as it strikes four in the afternoon we shall all be at the bull fight. I've been dreaming of it for a week. It is unlikely that I shall take an active part in the fight as I had originally intended. My idea was to stupefy the bull by showing him the third act of *Les Muscadins* and to finish him off by singing the third waltz. But my wife doesn't agree with these bold ideas of mine—she says I am just a dreamer.

If you see the director of the theatre at Port Said to whom M. de Lesseps strongly recommended me, tell him that I hope to let him have by the autumn the two first acts of *Arabi*. This work will be the crown of my career, my *Parsifal*. After the first night of *Arabi* I am going to rest and I shall certainly deserve it.

Well, for us three it's been a hell of a sweat on this earth, especially for C. It hurts me to think of it. No respite or peace for him. Please tell him, my good Enoch, that he's merely getting himself into a bad way. He gets up at 8, takes the train, walks from the Gare St Lazare to his office. As soon as he arrives he locks himself up for two hours with Ernest to go through the correspondence. Lunch is dealt with in another mere couple of hours—it's a wonder he doesn't choke—and before he's had time to digest his food he is burdened with two more hours of absorbing work. It's awful! Ernest won't be able to stand this for long but that doesn't matter, he's not a partner, he's a bachelor. There wouldn't be much left of Earnest, not to speak of your own people to whom please remember me. But the father of a family, a husband—that's serious! Embrace him for me and tell him to look after himself.

Cordial feelings to you four from us two.

TO MM. ENOCH AND COSTALLAT

Seville, October 21st 1882

Well, my dear fellows, we've seen these Andalusian dancers wriggling about like intoxicated snakes! Every evening we go to the *bailos flamencos* and sit among the *toreros* in their costumes: black felt hats slashed in the middle, jackets cut above the hips, and tight-fitting trousers showing up their muscular legs and their beautifully shaped figures. The gypsies sing their malagueñas or dance the tango, and then the manzanilla is passed round and everyone has to drink. Those eyes, those flowers in their lovely hair, those shawls around their waists, those feet that go on tapping their ever-changing rhythms, those quivering arms running down their supple bodies, and the wavy movements of their hands, those sparkling smiles and that marvellous Sevillian behind that goes on turning and turning while the rest of the body doesn't seem to move at all! *"Olle, Olle!"* they cry. *"Anda la Maria! anda la Chiquita! Eso es! Baile la Carmen, anda! anda!"* And while this is going on, two grave-looking guitarists, smoking cigarettes, scrape away something or other in triple time (only the tango is in duple time). The cries of the women excite the dancers, and when they get to the end of their dance they become literally mad with passion. You can't believe it! Last night two painters came with us and made sketches, and I took my music paper with me. We had all the dancers around us. The singers went over their songs for me, and when they left they did give us a hearty handshake—both Alice and me! Then we had to drink from the same glass. Ugh! it was disgusting! Well, we're none the worse off this morning. But you know I couldn't picture Mme Enoch here. And this is the kind of life we are going to lead for a month, until we get to Barcelona—having been to Malaga, Cadiz, Granada, Valencia! I shall be in a state of nerves! But we must see something before pegging out. You know, my dear chaps, if you haven't seen the swaying and singing dances of the Andalusian girls, singing in time too, while they shout *"Anda! anda! anda!"*, if you haven't seen this, you haven't seen anything. They have a marvellous trick of clapping a syncopated 3/4 while the guitarist goes on with a rhythm of his own, as if nothing were happening. Some of them clap the first beat of every bar *forte*, but each girl has a rhythm of her own, and the result is most curious. I'm noting it all down—but what a job! Then we go and see the cathedrals —they are magnificent—and the museums, and get lost in the streets, and eat ourselves sick, and don't get to bed before midnight. Yes, we're a silly pair. Whenever we feel

like it, up we go to the top of that damned *Giralda* from which
we have the most beautiful panorama in the world. I know the
names of all the bells, for I have made friends with the young
bell-ringer. His sisters dance at the *bailos* in the evening, and
during the day they act as guides at the cathedral. That's their
life! Beggars all over the shop, smoking cigarettes and most
dignified in appearance. They don't say "thank you" for what
they get; they think it is due to them. And all night long the
Sereno wanders through the town with his pikestaff and lantern
shrieking: *Ave Maria purissima*, etc.; that means that all is well
in the town and we can go to sleep. There's even a dance called
the *Sereno* in which the old watchman is taken off and the
dancer shrieks *Ave Maria purissima* at the top of her voice and
wriggles her behind. They are calling us to lunch—we all send
you a kiss.

TO MADAME ENOCH

Granada, November 4th 1882

My dear friend Madame Enoch,

I am happy to send you this letter from a town the name of
which suggests a flower which would go very well in your
hair. This vision of black ebony hair will follow me everywhere—and you should see it in Andalusia! Dragging each
other on, Alice and I find the days too short to look at all the
pretty women, not to speak of the men who have a jaunty way
with them, I can tell you. We roam around the tobacco works,
the cane-sugar factories, the café-concerts and the gypsy
haunts. If you want to track us down look for some place of
more or less ill-repute. And of course at every street corner there
is someone scraping away at a guitar. I'm not crazy about the
guitar. It's an instrument that takes fifty minutes to tune and on
which you accompany yourself for ten: in all, one hour.

This evening Don Antonio, captain of the Gypsies, is going
to treat us to a Flamenco show of his own. It'll probably be
pretty tough but with all we've seen over the last month I

don't think there is anything we need be afraid of. They're all right these Andalusians: their political outlook is based on the provision of a couple of guitars, five or six girls dancing, a package of cigarettes and a bottle of manzanilla.

I need hardly tell you that I'm going to put together for you a terrific malagueña—you'll sing it divinely. Spanish popular music is extraordinarily rich. I'm writing down everything I can lay my hands on and hope by the end of December to bring back some interesting sketches.

We have just left the Alhambra. Here you go to the Alhambra as in Paris you go to a café. What a wonderful place! When I come back I'll draw you some little sketches which may give you some kind of idea. Abu Abd Allah was a chap who certainly had a good time of it. The bathrooms, the perfume rooms, the swimming pools, the fountains, the couches, the summer houses, the big towers and the little towers, the nooks and corners—when in the midst of all this the sultanesses began to dance, perfume themselves and bathe, take a rest, sway their hips, dress and undress, well, it looks to me as if Boabdil must have had a very good time. A chemist (I don't want to disturb the picture) or rather the son of a chemist whom I met and who really plays the piano very well, is going to lug me off to see the local artists. He loves my *Pièces pittoresques* and I've promised to send them to him. He's a handsome dark chap of about eighteen or twenty, broad and strong, and who would certainly make his mark in Paris. He lent his grand piano to Rubenstein recently when he came to Granada to give two concerts. Captain Voyer played on a very different kind of piano when he gave concerts at Puerta Santa Maria near Cadiz. So we saw from the posters as we dragged ourselves through the streets of Puerta Santa Maria—every evening we count our ten toes to see whether we haven't left one behind. What is coarser than Spanish thread? The answer is the Andalusian pavements. What about carriages then, you may ask, dear lady. To go a couple of yards the cab-drivers ask five pesetas. They prefer to snore on their boxes rather than put themselves out. And the police? There aren't any.

But what a sky! And what a climate! We go about in drill clothes all day and the air is so transparent that you could almost touch the Sierra Nevada which is about ten miles away. We'll certainly have something to tell you when we get back. If you saw Alice in a mantilla and your humble servant in the three-cornered hat of a bullfighter you wouldn't easily recognise us. . . .

TO EDOUARD MOULLÉ

Granada, November 4th 1882

"There are too many flowers," said Granier somewhere or other; and in turn I repeat there are too many wonders. We are satiated, cloyed, drunk with masterpieces. It's certainly a wonderful country, this. The cathedrals of Burgos, Avila, Toledo and Seville, the museums of Madrid, the Carfuga of Miraflores, white Cadiz, radiant Malaga, and here the Alhambra, the Generalife, the Sierra Nevada—Cordoba which we are going to see in a few days, then Murcia, Valencia, Elche with its palm trees and Barcelona and Saragossa—we shall have seen everything, taken everything in, and in a month we shall have to leave this adorable country of Spain and say goodbye to the Spanish wenches—for all I propose to tell you about them now is that they're just right, these little monkeys. I haven't seen what you'd call an ugly woman all the time I've been in Andalusia. I'm not referring to their feet. They are so small that I've never seen them; but their hands are so pretty and dainty, and what shapely arms! In all this I'm only speaking of what is to be seen. . . . Then there are the ornaments, love-locks and other clever arrangements of their hair, the fan of course, a flower in the bun, a comb prominently displayed on the side, the flowery shawl in crêpe de Chine with a long fringe tied round the waist, bare arms, and eyes with lashes long enough to be curled, the mat white or orange

colour of their skin according to their race, and all these lasses
do nothing but laugh, throw their arms about, dance, drink and
wouldn't give a damn for our little village of Montceau-les-
Mines. There's Andalusia for you!

Every evening we roam round the café-concerts, Alice and I,
when they sing the Malagueñas, the Soledas, the Zapateados
and the Peteneras. The main thing about the dances is that they
are completely Arabian. If you saw them wriggling their
behinds, swaying their hips and writhing their bodies you
wouldn't want to be off in a hurry. At Malaga things got so
hot that I had to take my wife away; that was a bit too much.
I can't write to you about it, but it's not to be forgotten and
I'll tell you about it. I needn't tell you that I've copied down
masses of tunes; the tango, a kind of dance in which a woman
moves her behind like the pitching of a ship, is the only one in
double time; all the others are either in 3/4 (Seville) or 3/8
(Malaga and Cadiz); in the North they have something else, a
curious kind of 5/8. The 2/4 of the tango is always in the form
of a habanera. This is what happens: one or two women begin
dancing, two queer chaps scrape away something on tinny
guitars and five or six women bawl out in a screamingly funny
voice triplets which are impossible to note down for they keep
changing the tune, just snatches of a tune something like this:

You hear syllables, words, portamentos, then they begin
clapping and beating out the six quavers accentuating the
third and the sixth; and then come the shouts: "*Anda, anda! La
Salud! Eso es la Mariquita! Gracia, nationidad! Baila, la chiquilla!
Anda, anda! Consuelo! Olé, la Lola! Olé, la Carmen! Que gracia,*

que elegancia!" all this designed to excite the dancing girls—
it's simply staggering.

The Sevillana is quite different; this is a 3/4 something like
this (with castagnettes):

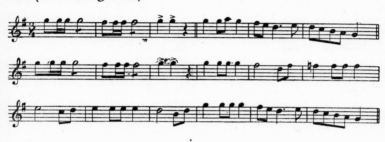

or you find:

All this looks absolutely extraordinary if you imagine two
love-locks, a pair of castagnettes and a guitar. The Malagueñas
can't really be written down. They are in the style of recitative
which has nevertheless a shape and which always ends on the
dominant. The guitar provides a 3/8 rhythm and there is an
old chap seated next to the guitarist with a stick between his
legs beating out, against the 3/8, a rhythm like this:

constantly syncopated. The women instinctively syncopate the
bars in a thousand different ways and manage while dancing

to beat out with their heels an incredible variety of rhythms. It's like this:

all this with their heels; it's a combination of rhythm and dance. The tunes scraped out on the guitar are of no interest. And anyhow you can't hear them what with the cries of *"Anda, Olé Olé, la chiquilla! que gracia! que elegancia! Anda! Olé! Olé la chiquirritita!"* And the more they shout the more the dancing girls laugh, show their teeth, sway their hips and writhe.

If you want me to tell you about a bullfight—we have about fifteen on our conscience—I must have advance notice at Poste Restante, Valencia, when I shall be happy to hear from you. . . .

TO MADAME EMMANUEL CHABRIER

La Membrolle, 1883

I feel I was born a native of La Membrolle, André too, also Nanine, we feel so much at home here. At 6.30 in the morning I take my shower in the stables; from 7 to 11 work, then lunch; from 1 to 6 work again; dinner, a walk round the garden, a ride on the top of the bus with the two dowagers, and at 9.30 to bed. I set all this down like an old schoolmaster. Nanon already knows everyone in the village. The day before yesterday we went to see the famous Baron de F.—a nice chap to be sure, but a thorough-going peasant. He goes about in a smock and clogs and so does his wife. . . .

There are here, I see them as I write, five wonderful trees, each six hundred years old: walnut trees with tremendous trunks, no I think they are chestnuts with enormous holes burrowed by rabbits and foxes, and higher up other strange openings where whole families of owls and bats make their home. In the spring, apparently, these trees give a protective covering to the love-making of all sorts of furry or feathered animals: they kiss, they go for each other, they squeal with their beaks, their snouts—all sorts of things. I stood there look-ing at these venerable trees whose roots have still enough strength and sap to bring forth young little chestnut trees which grow there under the wings of their great-great-grandfathers. What power! In the shade of such giants I don't think one could compose anything trivial. I must go and see them again. They are better than Massenet; they make me think of Father Bach who is still breeding new generations of musicians and will go on breeding them for ever.

TO M. COSTALLAT

1884(?)

Now here's another piece, the third [of the *Valses Roman-tiques* for two pianos]. . . . It's extremely clear this music, make no mistake about it, and you get your money's worth on the spot. It's certainly music of today, or tomorrow, but not of yesterday; so I think it will be a good and sensible idea to publish it. In ten years you'll see. . . .

What I can't write is any kind of sick music. There are a few young people among us, who torment themselves in getting three jaded chords out of their system, the same ones all the time. There's no life in it, no tune in it, they're not worth a rap. I try to tell them but they call me a *pompier*—a *pompier* if you please! . . . In the second ballad, the short piece, you must really sing. Now that there are no more square-cut songs

F

in opera we must find room for them somewhere. The ballad
is the form. At first sight I don't suppose you'll understand
anything of it. I'll play it to you in three weeks. Put it aside. . .

TO M. COSTALLAT

1886(?)

Obviously I am *vieux jeu* for the young masters of today,
very *vieux jeu*. So is Lalo and Franck himself. I want to go further and I think that really Wagner seems to them to be thread-
bare. What I am principally concerned with is to write what
pleases me and to show who I am; I must on no account be
boring. These young people all seem to be writing the same
music. Whatever name it appears under it comes from the same
shop. It's music in which they want to put everything, but in
which there is ultimately nothing. In ten years' time it will be
forgotten. . . . Incidentally the introductory chorus in F
from *Oberon* which I heard yesterday played by a local band at
Boulogne is absolutely eternal; it will last for ever. Actually
it is the structure of opera librettos that is now old-fashioned.
Since Meyerbeer it's always the same kind of libretto and we
have had enough of it. On the other hand, a musical conversation spread over four acts which is what is now required
becomes hopelessly monotonous. . . .

Berlioz, a Frenchman if ever there was one and who was
certainly not outmoded in his day, certainly found variety,
colour and rhythm in the *Damnation*, *Romeo* and *L'Enfance du
Christ*. But his works lack unity, they say. To which I reply:
Rubbish. If unity can only be achieved at the expense of
becoming a bore, well then I'd rather be two people, three,
four, ten, twenty; which is to say that I prefer to have ten
colours on my palette and merge together all the tones.
This means that I don't continually wish to write: 1. An introductory act; 2. An act for the old hens with vocal flourishes for
the queen; 3. The ballet act leading to a never-ending finale
and general confusion; 4. The love duet; and 5. The row just

before midnight, rifle fire and death of all the principal characters. . . . I want my music to be beautiful throughout, and there are many different forms of beauty. If the only colours I could use were grey pearl or canary yellow with their various shades, well no, I should not find them enough . . . even though there may be as many as three hundred varieties of grey pearl. Let's have a little red, good God! Down with the *Quiou-quiou*. We can't keep to the same colour. Variety, shape and life are what we want and above all an ingenuous simplicity if you can—that's the most difficult of all.

TO ERNEST VAN DYCK

La Membrolle, 1886

I have your letter at this very moment. I'm flabbergasted, delighted. Joy and astonishment at the same time! . . . A Knight of the Grail! He'll go to church, kneel before the holy altar and for the first time proclaim a resounding "Yes!" And now you can go bald, no one will mind in the least; to the monde and the demi-monde you will say your final farewell; you will have children, like me; love your wife, like me, and like me too, go on loving our silly music. For that's all we have: a wife, children and our silly music. . . .

Was it love at first sight? Tell me about it. Is your fiancée in London? You tell me nothing. "I'm getting married"—it takes my breath away. I have a chorus for the wedding day:

Voi - ci la jeu-ne fi-an-cé - e!

TO FELIX MOTTL

Tours, December 1st 1887

My dear Master,

Let me thank you for the kind interest which you have continuously shown in my work and allow me to tell you how grateful I am. I am looking forward to the honour of being performed at Karlsruhe and of being conducted there by you. Oh, you are thought a lot of here, I can tell you: when the name of Mottl is pronounced we bow very low. And the performance of my opera which I owe to my dear friend Van Dyck and to your devotion will be one of the most wonderful occasions of my life. In the meantime please thank Baron von Pudlitz whom I hope to meet personally.

I imagine you know the libretto of *Gwendoline*. It's a Danish legend arranged in very beautiful verse by Catulle Mendès who was closely connected with Wagner. And I may say that whatever merits it lacks, the libretto and the music of *Gwendoline* is the joint work of two fanatics of this great genius.

Van Dyck tells me that a translation is being made and that the work will be given in March or April. He also tells me—and this fills me with joy—that in August you will be good enough to give *Gwendoline* in Karlsruhe in the hope of attracting some of my compatriots.

Thank you for this kind thought. Between now and March I shall try and learn a few German words beyond *langsam*, *schnell*, *ausdrucksvoll* and *lebhaft*.

I hope I shall manage to speak at any rate a kind of pidgin German which may make everyone giggle but which I shall be able to get along with. During the later rehearsals I am counting on having an invigorating bath of *The Ring*. I know that at that time the four operas will be performed and that *Götterdämmerung* has been rehearsed. If you could include a certain score which is not yet worm-eaten, namely *Tristan*, then Chabrier would be in the seventh heaven. Let me know as soon as possible for throughout the winter I shall be on tenterhooks.

Of course I love my poor dear Paris—but here we only have two theatres, one for *La Juive*, the other for *Haydée*. That's hardly enough and between them these two theatres swallow up 1,300,000 frs. subsidy. Now and again, as if they were throwing a bone to a dog, they give a couple of acts of a ballet to some poor devil of a composer and this year it was old Ambroise Thomas who got the chance. It's no joke. As for earning a mere living, it's impossible unless you go in for operetta and then after ten years you have a fortune. But there's nothing doing for anyone who dreams of the lyrical drama, if he hasn't a well-lined purse. . . .

But I have courage and moreover this year, thanks to you, I shall have encouragement; my efforts will not have been in vain since you have accepted my dear little score which they find forbidding and muddled in my own country where they don't love music sufficiently—where they are too isolated.

By the side of our qualities—all peoples have their own—we have the great misfortune of being too prone to contemplate our navels and being too self-satisfied. Well, if anyone has the right to be satisfied it is I, and that I proclaim from the roof-tops and thank you most heartily.

TO MADAME EMMANUEL CHABRIER

Karlsruhe, February 15th 1888

Arrived here at 6.30 in the morning after a good dinner and a poor rest in the sleeping-car. After a good foot-bath and wash-up I went for a walk round the town. It's very prim, rather forlorn and clean: good well-to-do houses, the monotonous kind of German town which you know. It's cold but wonderful weather. On the horizon, the Black Forest.

At 10 we left our hotel. Mottl, Pabst—not one of them had called, though I had sent telegrams to them all. But none of these people get to bed before three in the morning and no one on earth can get them up before eleven.

At Mottl's place the servant said that he'd gone out. At Pabst's not a soul. Then we went to see Pudlitz at the theatre but there was no one there either; so I left my card.

Back at the hotel discovered that Mottl had sent a messenger to apologise. He was at home but asleep.

If that's their reception it's a bit chilly. I would have done better than that. His manners aren't up to mine. But I haven't come all this way to tell him as much and when I have the honour of meeting him I shall put on appropriate airs and graces. . . .

Apart from rehearsals of *The Ring*, all they are giving at the Opera until Friday are a number of foul operettas. Not much luck. All the same we'll go and hear tonight *The Trumpet of Salkingen* which is the local *Fille de Madame Angot*. . . . The women are ugly and dressed like guys. But the soldiers are terrific. . . .

TO MADAME EMMANUEL CHABRIER

Karlsruhe, February, 1888

At eleven o'clock we saw the famous Pudlitz at his room at the theatre. Everyone kow-tows to His Excellency. It's all settled and arranged. . . . Dinner at one. I told Mottl about our interview and he is going to hurry up this amiable but procrastinating old chap. After dinner Mottl asked us to his place. We played the overture four hands, the first chorus, the legend (which he finds admirably written) and the whole of the battle scene. He was transported and kept on saying: *Famos, famos.* . . . It's the first time Mottl has gone to such great expense for anyone. I think he's very sincere for he repeatedly said my music was original and individual. We left about half-past three, walked round the town and through the municipal gardens where the nobility, the townsfolk and the down-and-outs were merrily skating on the ice of the little lake.

. . . I wasn't invited to the reception of the Archduke, and a good thing too for at that time I shall be at the rehearsal of *Siegfried* which is quite another matter. We ran across the Archduke just now out for a brisk walk with his wife, the daughter of Wilhelm, and with a wolf-hound. He was in uniform, with the usual red-edged vizored cap, a long coat and the point of his sword reaching below it. He is a tall man over six foot, a long beard, erect and powerfully built. As he passes, the ordinary man in the street makes a low bow; the soldiers stop short and give a military salute. The women passers-by curtsy just as in a comic opera a young peasant girl might curtsy before a judge. It's most edifying. In all the public squares soldiers are at drill. They haven't time to put on weight; their job is more complicated than counterpoint.

TO FELIX MOTTL

La Membrolle, 1888

. . . I hear that you will be shortly leaving Karlsruhe and going to Vienna or Pesth. I shall be absolutely done for if you don't conduct my work at Karlsruhe! You, dear great artist, you and you alone are the person I want for I consider it a touching honour that you should rehearse and conduct my poor *Gwendoline*. Please don't leave me without any news. Within three weeks or a month be so good as to tell me if the chorus know their parts, if the producer, a fair chap with curly hair, very jolly and friendly, whose name I can't remember, is getting on with his difficult job. News, please, give me news! Doesn't matter if you write in German, I'll get it translated. You've got the entire orchestra, haven't you? As I can't get a performance here it's a matter of my personal pride. I shall invite *all* my Paris friends: Franck, Fauré, d'Indy, Lalo, Messager, Reyer, Widor—the whole lot will come to Karlsruhe. I want to make a nuisance of myself with the Paris theatres which won't hear of my work. Lamoureux has promised to come too—also at the appropriate moment I hope you'll inform the Kapellmeisters of round about: I should like Levi of Munich, whom I knew seven or eight years ago, to be there. I'll leave it in your good hands.

So, dear Mottl, don't leave your colleague and friend Chabrier, and believe that I shall always remember what a *man like you* has done for me.

TO ERNEST VAN DYCK

Paris, January 8th 1889(?)

I see from the papers that you are bawling out in *Lohengrin* and *Romeo* and even in *Carmen*. You've got there at last. Success, money! You're not yet thirty and you are at the height of your career. You're a healthy brute, you have a delightful wife, an adorable child. Good Lord, what a happy man! Come here, old boy, and let me put my arms round you. . . .

TO ERNEST VAN DYCK

Paris, January 8th 1889(?)

A year ago in Vienna when I saw Richter, to whom I played several extracts from *Le Roi malgré lui*, I thought they would produce it there. He said: "*Gwendoline* is very good but we've got so many operas of Wagner to play! There are plenty of Germans and Austrians who write music like that but they don't write comic operas with gay lively rhythms; they write either imitation Wagner or cheap operetta; and I believe (he went on) that the *Roi malgré lui* would have a great success here." The fact is that when I played him this confounded *Roi* he enjoyed himself no end. He really fell for the 2/3 sections. I have since written to him to recommend it (as he promised) but the old slacker has other fish to fry. So I let it go. But (and this is very confidential) if they have no inclination to produce Wagnerian works on the grounds that they have masses of them, why on earth do they want to put on *Le Chevalier Jean* of Joncières which is unbelievably old-fashioned? Also *Le Roi* is translated in German. . . you can get the libretto, *Der König wider willen* from Litolff. . . . I'm sure that in Vienna they would rather give *Le Roi* than *Gwendoline* and I believe you would pull it off, in view of Richter's interest, if you would take a hand in it. You have already brought me luck with *Gwendoline*. Come on, just give a thought to your old friend! It's not the right moment perhaps from my point of view because you are now going to be in the limelight, but you could blaze the trail and, on your return, tackle the matter seriously. What do you say, Romeo?

La Membrolle, June 13th 1889

My dear little Marcel,

Certainly I am glad to see that you are beginning to pay attention to your little girl friends. Women are created and brought into this world to earn our respect and to be loved. That we agree upon. But for the moment there is something else to be thought of too and that's your forthcoming exam. That's where I want you to divert your charm. If you want to please me let me see how winning you can be with your Latin translations and how tactful with Greek. Go on your bended knees before History and throw your kisses to Geography. Be courteous to Arithmetic and put your ardent passions into Composition.

So for the moment forget your little girl friends, and remember that if you are really thinking of your freedom in the future, for the next three or four years you will have to concentrate on your schoolwork. Of course we are delighted that you are apparently so attractive. But it is my duty to tell you what yours is.

Draw me a map of Germany showing the various kingdoms and duchies, the capitals and the main waterways, and send it on to me. Let's have each province, Baden, Bavaria, Wurtemberg, etc. marked out in red or blue pencil. Write to me often. You know how much I love you. . . . Kiss your dear mother for me and André and dear old Nanine.

TO MADAME EMMANUEL CHABRIER

La Membrolle, June, 1889(?)

What a wedding! I'll tell you all about it. Yesterday morning at 6.52 I picked up Alice at Mettray and we both arrived at Saint-Paterne on the stroke of eight. The old carriage was

waiting for us and in it was our old guy of an aunt. At half-
past eight we proceeded to Villebourg, and then from everywhere came the guests: Mme B. with her elder daughter
aged twenty, pretty smart, not bad-looking and intelligent.
And then all sorts of gushing folk. Cheeks kissed all round, we
are all pals together, and there is no end of fun. At ten o'clock,
the bride and bridegroom having tumbled out of their beds, we
are all counted and put in our places. A Monsieur G., a local
swell, acting as guide, offers his arm to Madame B. while I
grab his wife's and the procession starts in the burning morning
sun. Noses are poked out of the window all the way. Finally we
get to the town hall. G. and I are witnesses for the bridegroom.
We proclaim our names, Christian names, age, profession.
After the quaint ceremony of putting on the municipal sash,
performed as a duo by the Mayor and the schoolmaster, off
we go arm in arm again to the church. It's even hotter now,
and at the church door I break away from Mme G. and at the
request of the bridegroom I make a rush for the funny little
harmonium. The procession enters and I improvise a novel
introduction for the *Offertorium*, the *Elevation* and the *Agnus*.
Meanwhile the bridegroom's father, a cantor and another chap,
also a cantor, begin bawling out a strange mixture of *Kyries*.
I ended up by playing some kind of a little improvisation of my
own. It was twelve o'clock and getting hotter and hotter. We
were hungry and very thirsty. When we sat down to table there
were seventy of us. I was between the bride and Madame G.
We went on eating until three in an enormous barn not badly
got up for the occasion and it really wasn't at all bad. Between
each dish one of the young things had to get up and sing. Some
of them were so shy you couldn't hear a thing—they might
have been on the other side of the village. Their songs were
about swallows, green fields, woods and birds' nests—very nice
too. At three o'clock there was dancing, the bowling alley,
billiards and so on. I went on dancing wildly until eight
o'clock in the evening. Nothing could stop me. I danced with

young B., the bride and her sister, the daughter of N. (your old friend) who is very pretty, and many, many others. My shirt was dripping. At half-past eight, dinner. There were now a hundred of us and there was no holding us back: real old country fellows, the young things who sang their songs again about pretty birds, and then some of the men began to sing. One of them started singing *Le petit lapin de ma femme*. The pretty little B. knew what it was all about, split her sides and hid her face behind a serviette. At half-past eleven more dancing, I went for the girls like a young jaguar, but at 1.15 I slipped off, the schoolmaster took me to his home as agreed, brought me a nightcap and a nightgown and in a few minutes I was snoring like a trooper. The others didn't go to bed at all. This morning I was up at seven, fresh as a daisy and after a hearty breakfast at the C's and shaking hands with more than forty people, off I went in the little cart drawn by a black horse to the station at Dissay. And so eventually I got back to La Membrolle. . . .

Till tomorrow, my pet. A smacking kiss for everyone.

TO MADAME EMMANUEL CHABRIER

La Membrolle, April 26th 1890

Let me send you a kiss for our little pets and particularly for the one who tomorrow is performing his touching and human duty. [Marcel Chabrier's first communion.] Tell him to ask God in his prayers to protect us for we are only trying to do our best and are not really wicked. Tell him to pray for his mother's health and her sight, good school reports for his elder brother and for his old father a flow of inspiration and a little money. All this is rather a lot to ask for and in any case God has enough to do. But on the days of first communion I am sure that He makes a point of pricking up His divine ears so as to hear what the little ones whose hearts go out to heaven have to say and that He must appear to them as very kind and dear and homely. And children are so knowing! I am hoping with all my heart. . .

1890

Dear little Marcel,

Thank you for the letter you wrote me a few days ago and also for the one you are about to write, for M. Enoch has already told me about your visit to the zoo. It isn't a bad idea now and again to spend some time with animals; it's a change from human beings. But what you must always do is to think about what you see and never look at any object or animal without wondering what it is for or how it lives. At your age there is a lot to be learnt from an outing such as this; there's a great deal for your little mind to take in. So many people, who think themselves clever, go about looking at paintings, churches —they may even go for a walk in the country, attend special classes or spend an evening at the theatre—and they come home with nothing; they've seen nothing and nothing has entered their minds. They are like a flock of sheep and all they want to do is to while away the time until they come to the main event of the day which is dinner. Take to heart what I'm telling you here, for I really want you to develop this spirit of curiosity and it is now that your mind should be opened to the many worldly wonders.

TO MADAME EMMANUEL CHABRIER

La Membrolle(?), *May 9th* 1891

My dear wife,

I am grateful to you for what you are doing, but we shouldn't be content with just thanking ourselves. Duty comes first and there is nothing to be proud of in that. You speak of feelings of sadness; I have had these feelings longer than you, and if I appear to be cheerful to the outside world the reason is that my job demands it and that if I went about in any kind of a morose mood it would be the end. But there is a bigger question than this. We have no satisfaction from our children. I have done everything for them, shown them all the affection of which I am capable, been annoyed with them, angry, reasoned with them, reviled them, gone through the whole gamut of a father's feelings for his sons—and we have been gifted with two lazy-bones and not well either into the bargain. It's reasonable and perfectly natural to be worried when they are ill. But it would be equally desirable to take a firm hand with them and to let them think of the future. . . . There are times when a man like me who would have been glad to look after an off-spring teeming with life like their father, driven on by an ambition, any ambition—No, I give up! They have hardly enough brains in them for a dustman. It's heart-rending. . . . All I ask of you is to keep a watch on them; I have the right and the duty to ask as much from a mother anxious to fulfil her mission on this earth, and as for myself I need to have a reasonably clear head for a few years if I still want to do something useful. You have here a real part to play, and as I see it you owe this to our love. Read all this over; they are the words of a good man, a prophetic man who also sees far into the future. No more nonsense, no more squabbling. . . .

CLAUDE DEBUSSY

[1862-1918]

*Close on forty years after Debussy's death his pathetic and strangely
entangled life is still, to his biographers, mysteriously obscure. The
standard biography remains the monumental work of Léon Vallas,*
Claude Debussy et son temps, *published in English as* Claude
Debussy: His Life and Works *as long ago as 1933. When this
work appeared in France it was much maligned in certain quarters,
not because there was any question of the accuracy of its many re-
vealing facts, but because of the author's interpretation of them: it was
held that Vallas gave a one-sided view of Debussy's character,
particularly in regard to the latter part of his life. An interpretation of the unusual facts of Debussy's life is, for the biographer,
an extremely delicate task, and though many criticisms were justi-
fiably levelled at Vallas his far-reaching researches have invariably
served as the principal basis for the numerous biographies of Debussy
that have since been written. In the last twenty-five years various
minor biographical contributions have been made, but the work one
awaits with the keenest interest is the entirely new version of Vallas's
great study, completed before his death last year and shortly to be
published in France. It is expected that the new work will contain
many illuminating facts deliberately withheld by Vallas in his earlier
work as well as such new material as may now be disclosed.*

*In the meantime views on the relationship between Debussy's life
and his work must be expressed with caution. Yet even with the
documents now at our disposal it is becoming more and more evident
that there was in Debussy's character a terrifying* côté noir *that
would seem to rank him with the ghastly though magnificently idealistic figures of Gauguin and Verlaine. A philosophy veering from the
most indulgent hedonism to bitter disillusionment is frequently*

89

characteristic of the lives and works of poets and painters of this period. But among musicians, Debussy alone represents their counterpart. Hence the linking of Debussy's name with the Impressionist movement—a reasonable association in many respects though "Impressionism" was a word Debussy himself held in horror: "I am now writing something," he says of the orchestral Images *"which the fools will refer to as Impressionism—a word they have even applied to Turner, the greatest creator of mystery in art." In those words may be seen the explorer's instinctive recoiling at any suggestion of being himself discovered. The new worlds of Debussy, among the last of the new worlds which it has been given to musicians to discover, were in fact being fast invaded. Towards the end of his life he was himself being driven out of them by his imitators. The story of the young writer René Peter, who confided his concern at the growing number of Debussy's meretricious followers, ("Tu sais Claude, les Debussystes m'agacent." "Moi, ils me tuent!") illustrates an alarming phenomenon in the music of our time.*

The published correspondence of Debussy frequently allows a glimpse behind the screen of bristling irony by which the secretive composer obscured himself from the outside world. But even in reading his letters consecutively in the eight slender volumes so far published, one is aware of many disconcerting gaps. There are also, particularly in his letters to intimate friends, many strange undertones or laconic abbreviations which are difficult to evaluate. The conversational tone of these letters, like his music—seemingly improvised or drawn from the circumambient air—is not always to be taken on its face value. Quips about Wagner, for instance, the one figure that dominates his entire musical life, are simply meant to conceal the intensity and also the humility of his admiration. So it is with the veiled references to the terrible tragedy of his first marriage: his saturnine nature seemed generally to forbid any kind of development of human relationships.

The letters grouped together in the following selection are addressed to friends and associates with whom, for the most part, Debussy was only temporarily intimate. Alone the correspondence with the Swiss writer Robert Godet extends throughout his life. The architect

Debussy [*c.* 1892]
by Alexandre Steinlen

Debussy [*c.* 1905]
by Sacha Guitry

Monsieur Vasnier and the bookseller Emile Baron receive appeals from the revolutionary young Debussy from Rome. To Ernest Chausson and Eugene Ysaÿe he confides the anguish of bringing forth Pelléas et Mélisande. Perhaps the most intimate and affecting letters are those addressed to Pierre Louÿs, the pleasure-seeking décadent with whom he was constantly discussing plans for ballets and plays destined to come to nothing. Throughout Debussy's life there was constantly swarming in the back of his mind these plans, some of them apparently quite far advanced, which never materialised. He thus goes into great detail for a plan of an opera on As you like it *which had been adapted by Paul-Jean Toulet. To Messager, the first conductor of* Pelléas, *and André Caplet, his amanuensis of the later years, he confides his growing disillusionments. But these later years were also the most productive in Debussy's life. "I am writing down everything that comes into my mind, like a madman," he tells his publisher Jacques Durand. And as we may see from these pathetic letters, the sick and impoverished composer persisted to the last bitter days.*

G

DEBUSSY

TO M. VASNIER

Rome, 1885

HERE I am in this abominable Villa Medici. I can tell you that my first impressions are not very favourable. It's awful weather—rainy and windy. There was no need to come to Rome to have the same weather as in Paris, especially for anyone with such a grudge against Rome as I have.

My friends came to meet me at Monte Rotondo, where the six of us slept in one dirty little room. If you only knew how changed they are! None of their good-hearted friendly ways of Paris. They're stiff and impressed with their own importance—too much Prix de Rome about them.

In the evening when I arrived at the Villa I played my cantata, which was well received by some, but not by the musicians.

I don't mind. This artistic atmosphere and camaraderie that we are told about seem to me very exaggerated. With one or two exceptions, it is difficult to talk to the people here, and when I hear their ordinary conversation I cannot help thinking of the fine talks we used to have which opened my mind to so many things. Then the people here are so very egoistic. I've heard the musicians demolishing each other—Marty and Pierné against Vidal, Pierné and Vidal against Marty, and so on.

Ah! When I got back to my enormous room, where you have to walk a league from one piece of furniture to another, I felt so lonely that I wept! I'm so used to your friendship and to your asking me about my work. I shall never forget all you have done for me and the place I had in your family. I shall do all I can to prove to you that I am not ungrateful. So please don't forget me, for I feel that I am going to need you.

I've tried to work but I can't. You know how much I love music and how much this state of mind annoys me. This is not the life for me. Their happiness isn't mine. It's not pride that makes me hate this life. I can't get used to it. I have no feeling for it and I haven't the necessary indifference.

Yes, I fear that I shall have to return to Paris earlier than you think. It may appear silly, but what is there to do? I don't want to make you cross and I should be very sorry to try your friendship. But whatever you think, you can't accuse me of lacking courage. I'm rather unwell—Rome again—my beastly heart doesn't seem to be working properly. I rack my brain to work, but nothing comes of it except a fever which knocks me down completely.

I was so pleased to get your letter, and if I'm not asking too much, I know how little time you have, send me a long letter to remind me of the pleasant talks we used to have. . . .

Give my best regards to Madame Vasnier. How is Marguerite? Is she still working at my songs? I am very fond of Marguerite and I would like her to become an accomplished musician. That would please you and me too, for at least I should have done something worth while. A kiss for her and also for that silly little Maurice.

TO M. VASNIER
Rome, June 4th 1885

Many people have sung the praises of the Italian climate all of which strikes me, in my present mood, as somewhat ironic. I admit that your letter contains unanswerable arguments and the result is that I have not given way to my instinct to run away and that I am still here. Does this please you? Then let me expound on some of my ideas, it will remind me of the very pleasant times we had at our evenings together.

I've changed my mind regarding the first work I shall send to paris; it will not be *Zuleima*, as I had intended, for I no longer like it. These great silly verses, which are only great in

their length, bore me, and my music would be stifled by them.
Then there's another thing: I don't think I shall ever be able
to put music into a strict mould. I'm not speaking of musical
form; it's a literary question. I shall always prefer a subject
where, somehow, action is sacrificed to feeling. It seems to me
that music thus becomes more human and real and one can
then discover and refine upon a means of expression.

I don't know whether I've spoken to you of *Diane au Bois* of
Théodore de Banville. I imagine I have, and this will be the
text of my first work. *Diane* isn't a bit like the poems that are
generally used for these *envois,* which are really only highly
polished cantatas. Thank God! I had enough of one of them and
I think I should take advantage—as you would say—of the only
good thing there is at the Villa, the liberty to work and do
something original instead of always keeping to the old paths.
I'm sure that the Institute won't be of my opinion. Their way,
of course, will be the only right one! But I'm too fond of my
freedom. At least if they don't allow me to go where I like, I
can think and do what I like. All I can say is that I can't write the
kind of music they would approve. Now, I don't know if
I'm big enough to do what I have in mind. Anyhow, I'll do
all I can to make some of them content, the rest can go
hang . . .

TO M. VASNIER

Rome, November 24th 1885
I want to tell you about the only time I have been out this
month. I went to hear two masses, one of Palestrina, the other
of Orlandus Lassus, in a church called S. Maria dell' Anima. I
don't know if you know it—it is stuck away among some awful
little streets. It appeals to me very much, as it is very simple and
pure in style, unlike so many others with their array of sculp-
tures, pictures and mosaics all so theatrical. The statue of
Christ in these churches looks like a lost skeleton that wonders
how it got there. The Anima is the only place to hear such

music, which is the only church music there is for me. That of Gounod and company seems to come from some kind of hysterical mysticism and has the effect of a sinister farce.

The two above-named people are masters, especially Orlandus, who is more decorative and more human than Palestrina. The effects he gets from his great knowledge of counterpoint are amazing. You perhaps don't know that counterpoint can be the nastiest thing in music, but in their work it is beautiful.

TO EMILE BARON

November 6th 1886

Would you believe me if I told you that I find Rome more and more positively ugly? It's amazing how unlikeable I find this town of marble and fleas. It's all fleas and ennui. The Villa Medici is still the sort of factory of moribund products that I have often described to you. So we needn't speak of that any more. But I've changed my room, and I have now the pleasure of seeing the Roman men and women who pass before my window and the long processions of priests some of whom, dressed in black, are like curious black radishes and others, in red, like roguish pimentos. It's exactly like certain extraordinary pictures in which you see vegetables of all sorts of fantastic shapes and sizes scattered far and wide. . . .

TO EMILE BARON

Rome, 1887 (*winter*)

You mentioned in your letter how much you wanted to go to a town where it was always spring. Well, don't come to Rome, because at present this town, reputed to be so sunny, is like Moscow, all covered with snow and freezing cold. The Romans don't seem to be able to make it out. The coats they wear are too short in any case, and they don't seem to be able to get used to proper overcoats. But the snow gives a very pretty colour to the ruins. It shows up their severe contours and makes them look clean. They are a thousand times better than with that perpetual blue sky and their usual pipeclay colour . . .

TO EMILE BARON

Rome, 1887

I believe that the public, apart from the shopkeepers who form the large part of it, have had enough of cavatinas and *pantalonnades* which show up the singer's fine voice and form. It is curious that the literary movement has found such support —the new forms of the Russian novelists, for instance (I wonder they haven't placed Tolstoy higher than Flaubert), while there is no sign of music changing at all. A dissonant chord would almost cause a revolution.

TO M. VASNIER

1887

You know when I work how doubtful I am of myself. I need someone on whom I can count, to give me strength. When something of mine pleased you it gave me courage. Here I should never have that. My friends make fun of my sadness and I should never get any encouragement from them. If things don't go better I know that many people will give me up. But I'd rather do twice as much work in Paris than drag out this life here. . . .

I am leaving on Saturday and shall arrive in Paris on Monday morning. Don't, I beg of you, be too hard with me. Your friendship will be all I have.

TO ROBERT GODET

December 25th 1889

I am so glad, dear friend—just allow my little sensibility to speak awhile—yes, I am so glad of our friendship, over which thoughtless pride had cast its shadow—and I am glad too that such pain as we have known has been shared. All this is perhaps an old-fashioned way of looking at life. But then fortunately we are not "modern"! . . .

Such music as mine has no other aim than to become part of things and people. That you have accepted it is a more lovely glory than any of the elegant people who kow-tow to the Wagnerian Monsieur Lamoureux with his eyeglasses and hieratic forefinger. . . .

There was a gathering of a few people at Le Mercier's to hear two extracts of *Endymion* translated from Keats. They were very beautiful once you accept his tone and atmosphere: watery landscapes and a very casual Diana instead of a clearly marked character.

I saw your friend D. who struck me as a delightfully simple-minded fellow with a lovely smile on his face. As a translator Le Mercier strikes me as being far superior to the other Mercier we know—as a rule he speaks in riddles. . . . Then of course we went to Vachelle's where Jean Moréas championed the cause of Schopenhauer without anyone provoking him to do so—I wonder why he did? Whereupon Le Mercier attacked him whilst D. continued to keep that smile on his face, the only reasonable thing, in the circumstances, to do.

TO ROBERT GODET

February 13th 1891

I am sorry not to have been near you, but recently I have been so afraid of myself that all you might have seen was a soul in distress. Silence, I thought, was preferable, though if we had been able to have a heart-to-heart talk I should have told you about my troubles and my sufferings. To tell you about it all choosing the right words would either be rather meaningless or unnecessarily bombastic. But I did miss you! So do please forgive this silence on my part which was not in itself real, for I was bursting to say everything. In truth I am still much distressed, for the unexpected and sorry end of the episode I told you about brought some bad words between us. I had the strange experience then, as those hard words fell from her lips, of hearing too, at that very moment, the most touching and beautiful things she had said. The result was that I felt powerless and torn to pieces by the discord of reality tending to obliterate the ringing memory of her voice living still within me. I had to face reality in the end, but I have left much behind me and it will be some time before I can find salvation in work. . . . Though I still don't know whether she possessed what really I was looking for—*Le Néant*, possibly, in the end—I am nevertheless mourning the disappearance of the dream of a dream. . . .

TO ERNEST CHAUSSON

Paris, May 21st 1893

I'm rid of the *Rheingold*. This is a nuisance so far as the gold is concerned, but it is good to have done with the Rhine. The last performance was a terrible bore. Catulle Mendès spoke on *Die Walküre* in such a way that the mothers who had naïvely brought their daughters were frightened away by the wicked priest's fiery words. The month of May, it appears, is henceforth to be the month of *Die Walküre*, for some simple-minded people believe that this work announces the spring of a new music and the death of the old worn-out formulæ. It's not what I think, but that doesn't seem to matter.

TO ERNEST CHAUSSON

Paris, June 4th 1893

Ah, my dear friend! What a Sunday! A joyless Sunday it was without you. Had you been here the atmosphere would have been a delight to breathe, for I must tell you that if I had already loved you greatly the few days I spent in your company would have made me ever your devoted friend. But I will not try to express my emotions here. However lyrical I might become I should not do myself justice.

Yet this is not so laughable as you might think. It was so good to feel that I belonged somehow to your family and that I was part of you all. But am I not going too far, and won't you feel my friendship to be rather a nuisance? I wish so much to please you that sometimes I imagine things that, decidedly, are crazy. . . .

TO ERNEST CHAUSSON

Paris, September 6th 1893

Whatever I do I have not been able to enliven the mournful scene of my life: some of the days I have passed, murky, tragic and silent, are like those of a hero of Edgar Allan Poe; and my romantic soul is like a Ballade of Chopin! When I am alone too many memories crowd into my mind which can't be dismissed as easily as that and I must thus go on living and waiting. . . .

Here I am, just turned thirty-one and not quite sure of my æsthetic. There are still things that I am not able to do—create masterpieces, for instance, or be really responsible—for I have the fault of thinking too much about myself and only seeing reality when it is forced upon me and then unsurmountable. Perhaps I am rather to be pitied than blamed. In any case I am writing you this expecting your pardon and your patience.

I had a visit from Henry de Régnier who is most fond of you—which is rather like talking of rope in the house of a man who has been hanged. Accordingly I was as pleasant to him as possible and played *L'Après-midi d'un faune* which he finds as warm as the inside of an oven though he likes the shimmering feeling in it too (they don't seem to go together). But when he speaks about poetry he is highly interesting and reveals an acute sensitiveness. . . .

Received a very friendly letter from Vincent d'Indy and praises that would bring blushes to the lilies held in the hands of the Blessed Damozel. . . .

Latest news: C. A. Debussy finishes a scene of *Pelléas et Mélisande* ("A fountain in the park", Act IV, scene iv), on which he would like to have the opinion of E. Chausson. It has been suggested to run excursion trains between Paris and Royan [where Chausson was staying], in view of this event, of which there is no further need to mention the importance.

TO ERNEST CHAUSSON

Paris, 1893

The person I was most interested to see there [Brussels] was Ysaÿe, whom I called on first. You won't be very surprised to hear that he actually shrieked with joy on seeing me, hugging me against his big chest and treating me as if I were his little brother. After which reception I had to give him news of every one and particularly of you, of whom, unfortunately, my only knowledge was from letters. And then music, and music till we went mad with it. That memorable evening I played in succession the *Cinq Poèmes* [of Baudelaire], *La Damoiselle élue* and *Pelléas et Mélisande*. I got as hoarse as if I had been selling newspapers on the street. *Pelléas* softened the hearts of certain young people, English, I believe; as for Ysaÿe, he became delirious. I really can't repeat what he told me! He liked your Quartet too and is getting some people to work at it.

I saw Maeterlinck, with whom I spent a day in Ghent. At first he assumed the airs of a young girl being introduced to her future husband, but after some time he thawed and was charming. When he spoke of the theatre he seemed a very remarkable man. As for *Pelléas*, he authorized me to make any cuts I like and even suggested some important and useful ones himself. He says he knows nothing about music and when he comes to a Beethoven symphony he is like a blind man in a museum. But really he is a very fine man and speaks of extraordinary things in a delightfully simple way. When I thanked him for entrusting me with *Pelléas* he insisted that it was he who should be grateful to me for setting it to music. As my opinion was the very opposite I had to use what little diplomacy nature had endowed me with.

So, you see, it was a more profitable journey than the journey of Urien. [*Le Voyage d' Urien* was one of the first works of André Gide.]

TO ERNEST CHAUSSON

October 2nd 1893

I was in too great a hurry to crow about *Pelléas et Mélisande*, for after a sleepless night, in which I began to see things clearly, I had to admit that what I had got wasn't right at all. It's like a duet by Mr. Anybody-you-like; and then the ghost of old Klingsor, alias R. Wagner, appeared at a turning of one of the bars, so I tore the whole thing up and struck off on a new line with a little compound of phrases I thought more character-istic—trying to be both Pelléas and Mélisande. There is music behind all those veils by which she hides herself from even her most ardent worshippers. I've got something which will please you perhaps—the others I don't care about. Quite spontaneously I have used silence as a means of expression (don't laugh). It is perhaps the only means of bringing into relief the emotional value of a phrase. If Wagner used silence, I should say it was only in an extremely dramatic way, rather as it is used in certain other dubious dramas in the style of Bouchardy, d'Ennery and others!

TO ERNEST CHAUSSON

1894

Dear Friend,

It's Mélisande's fault—so will you forgive us both? I have spent days in pursuit of those fancies of which she is made. I had no courage to tell you of it all—besides, you know what such struggles are. I don't know if you have ever gone to bed, as I have, with a strange desire to cry, feeling as if you had not been able to see during the day some greatly loved friend. Just now I am worried about Arkel. He is from the other side of the grave and has that fond love, disinterested and far-seeing, of those who will soon disappear—all of which has to be said with *do ré mi fa sol la si do*. What a job!

I shall write to you at greater length tomorrow. This is just for you to know that I am thinking of you and to wish you good day.

TO EUGÈNE YSAŸE

September 22nd 1894

I am working at three *Nocturnes* for violin and orchestra. The orchestra of the first part consists of strings; of the second, flutes, four horns, three trumpets and two harps; of the third, of both of these groups. It is, in short, an experiment with the different combinations that can be obtained from one colour—like a study in grey in painting. I hope this will appeal to you, for the pleasure it might give you is what I am most concerned with. I am not forsaking *Pelléas* for this—and I must say that, the further I go, the more depressed and anxious I become. . . .

TO EUGÈNE YSAŸE

October 13th 1896

Dear great Friend,

I was most touched by your kind letter and your friendly anxiety for *Pelléas et Mélisande*. The poor little creatures are so difficult to introduce into the world, for with a godfather like you the world doesn't want to have anything to do with them.

Now I must humbly tell you why I am not of your opinion about a performance of *Pelléas* in part. Firstly, if this work has any merit, it is in the connection between the drama and the music. It is quite obvious that at a concert performance this connection would disappear and no one could be blamed for seeing nothing in those eloquent "silences" with which this work is starred. Moreover, as the simplicity of the work only gains significance on the stage, at a concert performance they would throw in my face the American wealth of Wagner and

I'd be like some poor fellow who couldn't afford to pay for "contra-bass tubas"! In my opinion Pelléas and Mélisande must be given *as they are*, and then it will be a matter of taking them or leaving them, and if we have to fight, it will be worth while.

TO PIERRE LOUŸS

February 9th 1897

My dear Pierre,

I fancy you must either be cursing me or have put me out of mind altogether. Whatever you feel, forget all about it. You haven't been out of my thoughts at all; in fact you've been very near me indeed. But of course if you will go off to places like Algeria. . . .

I've had some troublesome business in which Bourget seems to have joined forces with Xavier de Montépin—which may be not altogether impossible. Gaby, with her steely eyes, found a letter in my pocket which left no doubt as to the advanced state of a love affair with all the romantic trappings to move the most hardened heart. Whereupon—tears, drama, a real revolver and a report in the *Petit Journal*. Ah! my dear fellow, why weren't you here to help me out of this nasty mess? It was all barbarous, useless and will change absolutely nothing. Kisses and caresses can't be effaced with an india-rubber. They might perhaps think of something to do this and call it The Adulterer's India-Rubber!

On top of it all poor little Gaby lost her father—an occurrence which for the time has straightened things out.

I was, all the same, very upset and again very sad to feel you so far away, so hopelessly far away that I hadn't the strength to pick up my pen and write to you. I didn't think I could give you the right feeling of the thing. For writing is not the same as looking into the face of a friend. You will think perhaps: "It's his own fault." Well, there you are. I am sometimes as sentimental as a *modiste* who might have been Chopin's mistress. I must say that my heart is still capable of fluttering instead of getting on quietly with its own business . . . Now don't let us speak of this any more, and believe me to be still your fine strong Claude.

You must have heard all about the banquet in honour of Mallarmé. I was thoroughly bored and so, it seems, was Mallarmé who made an awkward little speech in sorrowful puppet-like tones. Francis Viélé-Griffin went about like a police-man and young Ernest La Jeunesse looked like some kind of a disease. I met there José-Maria de Hérédia who made no im-pression on me whatever.

The symphony of Dukas played by the orchestra was disap-pointing. It shrank to nothing and was like a mixture of Beethoven and Charpentier. It meant nothing to me at all.

Have you by the way done any work on the libretto of *Cendrelune*? I really don't deserve it. But you would really be helping me in giving me something to do and taking me away from all my troubles. . . .

Forain has suggested my writing the music, as you are aware, for his wife's pantomime. Do you know it? It's not at all bad, but not finished. I've been rather imposed upon, and I don't know how to get out of it unless I explain to her that she really hasn't got very far with it.

Let me have your reply, and your pardon, before long.

TO PIERRE LOUŸS

March 9th 1897

My dear Pierre,

Forgive me once again for this delay in replying to your two letters. And first let me tell you how delighted I am to see you better. I was worried about your being ill so far away and all alone—and here was I, a pitiful little pianist unable to afford any kind of long journeys of this kind. Otherwise I should have been playing the part of a modern Isolda who would have come to tell you that friendship can always be trusted. Anyhow my hope is that by the time this reaches you you will be yourself again and ready to go on with your musical work.

I haven't got any further than you with the score of *Messidor*, for life is short and I'd rather go to a café or look at pictures. How do you expect people so ugly as Zola and Bruneau to be capable of anything but the second-rate? Have you noticed, in their two articles, the deplorable use they make of patriotism? It might be bad, but in any case it's French!!! By George! We've only got one musician who's really French, and that's Paul Delmet. He's the only one who has caught the melancholy atmosphere of the faubourgs and the whole-hearted sentimentality round where that burnt grass is by the fortifications. The best disciple of this master is Massenet. The others with their social preoccupations and their claim to put life into chords of the seventh are just a lot of dreary fatheads. If, indeed, they have any view of life at all, it is through their last laundry bill.

I want these few lines to reach you as soon as possible and to bring you my friendly thoughts. More tomorrow.

Thanks and sweet smiles from Gaby.

March 27th 1898

Dear Pierre,

. . . I have been very unhappy since you left, unhappy in the bottom of my soul, and I have often found myself weeping, an utterly natural act by which you are suddenly united to the whole of humanity. . . .

I have of course done very little work, for music cannot be written under such circumstances. However the *Chansons de Bilitis* are finished, and I hope you will find that the third has some of the graces of the other two.

The three *Nocturnes* reflect my present mood; at first I had great hope in them, then I went through a period in which I felt just the opposite, and now I find them absolutely empty. I have never really been able to do anything whenever anything striking happens in my life; and it is precisely for this reason that I feed on memory. Some worthwhile feelings can be cultivated in this way: tears shed in the course of creating a masterpiece are nothing but nonsense.

It would be most kind of you to work at *Cendrelune*. I really need something to hold on to, to love, or I shall just go silly and might as well commit suicide which would be sillier still. I am not telling you all this just to make an effect; there are really times when I fear that I am losing whatever qualities I might have had. . . .

TO PIERRE LOUŸS

(? *April*) 1898

I really do need your affection, I feel so lonely and helpless. Nothing has changed in the black background of my life and I hardly know where I am going if it is not towards suicide— a senseless ending to something that might have turned out better. I've got into this state of mind from continually fighting against silly and despicable impossibilities. You know me better than anyone and you alone can take it upon yourself to tell me that I am not altogether an old fool. . . .

May 16th 1899

My dear Pierre,

You have certainly written the most wonderful books of the *fin de siècle* but there is an even more staggering wonder in the work of which you send me the first chapter this morning and for which you are asking the delightful co-operation of Mademoiselle Louise de Hérédia.[1]

[1] This letter was written in reply to the following letter from Pierre Louÿs:

May 15th 1899

My dear Claude,

Because of a love of those rich rhymes which she has no doubt acquired from her father, Mlle Louise de Hérédia is exchanging her name for that of Louise Louÿs which is more symmetrical and shapely. Which explains why I haven't seen you for so many days and nights.

The wedding will take place at Saint-Philippe in six weeks' time. Do

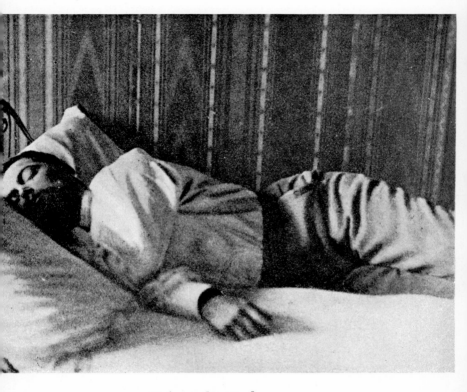

Debussy [*c.* 1895]
Photograph by Pierre Louÿs

Ravel conducting [c. 1930]
Drawing by Luc-Albert Moreau

Allow me to tell you how happy I am at this news and hope you will believe that my good wishes are perfectly genuine.

I haven't the honour of knowing the organist who is entrusted with providing harmonious music for the congregation at Saint-Philippe, but I shall certainly undertake to write the two hundred bars you ask me for. If they do not turn out to be very beautiful, they will at least express my friendly feelings and also an attempt at conveying a certain feeling that I have not expressed before. I don't know whether it will be strictly nuptial; the trouble is that I've been living in sin with Music for too long. . . .

Take for yourself my affectionate embraces and offer, I beg you, my respects and my devotion to the future Madame Louise Louÿs.

TO ROBERT GODET

January 5th 1900

I must tell you straight away of what has happened. Two things: I've moved and I've married. Yes, my dear friend, and please remain seated. Mlle Lily Texier has changed her disharmonious name to Lily Debussy, much more pleasant-sounding, as everyone will agree. She is unbelievably fair and pretty, like some character from an old legend. Also she is not in the least "modern-style". She has no taste for the music that Willy approves, but has a taste of her own. Her favourite

---

you know the organist of this strange place? My idea is to suggest to him a little Sebastianbacchic programme which might be introduced by the celebrated and unpublished *Hochzeitmarsch* of Debussy. Would you be inclined to write out two hundred bars for two keyboards and pedals [i.e. the organ at the church at Saint-Philippe du Roule] in the unusual rhythm of a march in four time—a piece of rather pompous character, also lewd and ejaculatory as one expects music to be at nuptial processions? One of thoes little masterpieces that you can turn out any day of the week after your whisky and while you are waiting for the first bottle. You wouldn't refuse to do this for an old friend, would you?

H

song is a roundelay about a grenadier with a red face who wears his hat on one side like an old campaigner—not very provoking æsthetically.

I have started working again, a piece of discipline to which my mind, choked up with heavy boredom, has not been in the least accustomed. I am working at *La Saulaie* [Willow-wood] on a poem of D. G. Rossetti which I have surely mentioned to you. It's very lovely and very alive; it is something which I almost make part of myself.

I have finished the *Trois Nocturnes* of which you know some sections. I feel sorry that you won't be here for the first performance which will take place in a few weeks. If you had been able to come, the occasion would at least have had some reason —things sometimes follow each other in life in the most odd way. . . .

TO PIERRE LOUŸS

February 6th 1900

Dear Pierre,

I have been to the show of the Charpentier family, so that I am in just the right state of mind to appreciate the forcefulness of your letter. It seems to me that this work had to be. It supplies only too well the need for that cheap beauty and idiotic art that has such an appeal. You see what this Charpentier has done. He has taken the cries of Paris which are so delightfully human and picturesque and, like a rotten "Prix de Rome", he has turned them into sickly cantilenas with harmonies underneath that, to be polite, we will call parasitic. The sly dog! It's a thousand times more conventional than *Les Huguenots*, of which the technique, although it may not appear so, is the same. And they call this Life. Good God! I'd sooner die straight away. What you have here is something of the feeling after the twentieth half-pint, and the sloppiness of the chap who comes back at four in the morning, falling all over the road-sweeper and the rag-and-bone man. And this man

imagines he can express the soul of the poor! It's so silly that
it's pitiful.

Of course M. Mendès discovers his Wagner in it and M.
Bruneau his Zola. And they call this a real French work!
There's something wrong somewhere. It's more silly than
harmful. But then people don't very much like things that are
beautiful—they are so far from their nasty little minds. With
many more works like *Louise* any attempt to drag them out
of the mud will completely fail.

I assure you that I'd very much like *Pelléas* to be played in
Japan, for our fashionable eclectics might approve of it—and I
can tell you that I should be ashamed.

Thank you for your kind and lovely letter, and *à bientôt*, eh?

August 25th 1900

My dear Pierre,
   Forgive the delay in replying to your very nice letter; my
excuse is simply some very sad news: Lily has spent some time
at a clinic and was operated on a few days ago. And nor is that
all. Apparently her whole system is affected and, confidentially,
tubercles are beginning to form at the top of her two lungs.
We must act quickly and send her to the Pyrenees for three or
four months. You can imagine how upset we shall be, not to
speak of the frightful material state in which we have long been.
Sometimes I really don't know which way to turn.

   I hope your stay at that dull place La Bourboule will have
done you some good—you must really follow your diet
unrelentingly—and don't think that I'm lecturing you merely
because I am older. You have too much to say to allow yourself to be prevented by illness. . . .

TO RAOUL BARDAC

Bichain, August 31*st* 1901

Dear Friend,
   My delay in replying in no way means that I was untouched

by the delicate attention of your letter. But here in Bichain, where I am sorry that we shall not see you, the minutes pass, one knows not exactly how.

I have the feeling of being at the other end of the world from Paris. The beastly fever that worries us all more or less, can't play havoc here, and there's no mistaking that the movement of the trees against the river-banks forms a counterpoint less poor than ours. . . . But the people are much less lovely than their setting. I needn't tell you that *le geste auguste du semeur* is quite forgotten and that when the angelus gently orders the fields to sleep you never see anyone striking that solemn pose of the lithographs.

What you tell me of X. . . . is most praiseworthy. One can never spend too much time constructing that special atmosphere in which a work of art should move. I believe that one should never hurry to write but leave everything to that many-sided play of thoughts—those mysterious workings of the mind which we too often disturb, prompted (though we may not like to admit it) by materialism and even cowardice.

Thank you for the Quartet. I shall be much indebted to you and don't know how I can repay you. Anyhow you can always count on me—for whatever that is worth, for I don't ever expect to become a big pot. I am far too unconcerned about my fellow beings, which is incidentally the only way to choose between them.

I shall be in Paris about 10th September and am afraid of being worried by more people than usual. But if you will come and see me it will make me forget how tiring they are.

TO ROBERT GODET

June 13th 1902

It is I, Claude Debussy, and I am none the prouder for being he. You will never know what remorse I feel for this unmentionable behaviour to you—you whom I love with all my heart! Truth to tell, I am tired out. It is like neurasthenia—a fashionable illness to which I thought I was immune. Apparently the mental and nervous strain of these last months has got the better of me, for I couldn't even think of writing to Godet. I have just now a moment when I feel less fagged and I beg you not to think too badly of me and to believe that there's nothing rotten in the state of Denmark. As for your article, I can hardly thank you, it would almost be an insult. Besides, I did not need to be reminded of your sensitive understanding and your scrupulously loyal love of beauty. . . . To come back to the story, I must tell you that the dress rehearsal has given me the most wretched trouble. What I foresee is that I shall continually be pushed into public life. I am not really made for that kind of thing and all I shall be is my clumsy self. . . .

Well, I am anxious to see these performances of *Pelléas* over. It's time they were. They are beginning to take it for one of the repertory works. The singers are beginning to improvise and the orchestra is getting heavy. They'll soon be thinking of *La Dame blanche* when they give it. . . . But I think I've got some way of getting the orchestral score published.

I will write to you shortly when I am in less of a hurry. I want this to reach you as soon as possible.

TO ANDRÉ MESSAGER

June 18th 1902

I suppose I had to expect the consequences of such excitement —I fell into an awful state of depression. The performance [of *Pelléas*] last Saturday didn't go off very well. All sorts of silly little things happened which really had nothing to do with me. There'll be another performance next Thursday unless something unfortunate happens in the meantime. I am quite incapable of putting a good face on things when I am ¬iscouraged, as you know. . . .

TO ANDRÉ MESSAGER

June 28th 1902

So Madame Raunay might sing the rôle of Pelléas next season. It may seem strange but it's not altogether silly.

According to Carré this idea occurred to him following a conversation he had with Madame Raunay in which she confessed to a mad love for Pelléas—a kind of lyrical masturbation it seems, or at any rate a form of narcissism.

In fact Pelléas has not the ways of making love of a hussar, and when he finally does resolve upon something his plans are so quickly checked by the sword of Golaud that the idea might be worth considering. I must admit that I would rather like to see. . . . Without speaking of the change in sex there would be a change in the scheme of timbres which worries me rather. Perhaps I am more curious about it than genuinely interested. I will await your advice.

TO PAUL-JEAN TOULET

October 21st 1902

Now let us talk of good Monsieur William. The second plan [for an opera on *As you like it*] you sent me suits me in every way. Don't you think we might heighten the interest of the first scene by the introduction of a choir off-stage which would comment on the various incidents of Orlando's wrestle? They would have exclamations to sing such as "He's down! No, he's not! Ah! He's no coward!" But, all joking apart, I think that musically it will be quite original. And I would like to have some of the songs sung by a group of people. The Duke is rich enough to have the Chanteurs de Saint-Gervais [a well-known choral society] and their conductor come to the Forest of Arden. We must find some pretty ceremonial for the betrothal and have it all end happily. Whenever you can replace the exact word by its lyrical counterpart don't hesitate. That doesn't mean that the tone in which the two scenes are

written doesn't please me. Quite the contrary. I suggest it
because of your fear of being too rhythmical. . . .

I have an idea which I offer to you for what it is worth.
Couldn't we use the scene between Charles the wrestler and
Oliver (Shakespeare scene i) as an introduction?

Send me everything you can before you leave. I'm convinced
we've got hold of something really admirable.

TO ANDRÉ MESSAGER
September 12*th* 1903

You perhaps do not know that I was destined for the fine
life of a sailor and that it was only by chance that I was led
away from it. But I still have a great passion for the sea. You
will say that the ocean doesn't wash the hills of Burgundy and
that what I am doing might be like painting a landscape in a
studio. But I have endless memories and, in my opinion, they
are worth more than reality, which generally weighs down
one's thoughts too heavily.

I mustn't be in too much of a hurry to declare that I
have finished *Le Diable dans le beffroi.* The scenario is more
or less finished and I have pretty well settled on the particular musical mood I want. But there will still be many sleepless nights, and just a hopeful question mark at the end of
it all.

As for the people who so obligingly tell me that I shall never
get beyond *Pelléas,* they can see no further than their noses.
They apparently do not realise that if ever anything like that
were to happen I should immediately turn myself into an
amateur horticulturalist or something of the sort. For I consider the most shameful thing is to repeat what one has already
done. Possibly these same people will find it scandalous that
I should abandon the shadowy Mélisande for the ironic capers
of the Devil and will accuse me once again of just being
outlandish. . . .

I embrace you affectionately,

TO M. CLARK,

DIRECTOR OF THE COMPAGNIE FRANÇAISE DU GRAMOPHONE

February 21st 1904

Monsieur,

The Gramophone appears to me, as to all who have heard it, a marvellous instrument. Moreover, music is assured by means of the gramophone of an immortality that is both complete and faithful in every way. It is therefore indispensable.

Yours truly,

C. D.[1]

---

[1] According to Henri Borgeaud, the editor of the Correspondence between Debussy and Pierre Louÿs, the above letter inspired the following skit sent by Louÿs to Debussy in March 1904:

The Gramophone and Claude Debussy

Following our policy of providing our readers with testimonials from the Great Instruments of Music, we offer them to-day an interview with the Gramophone.

This young instrument, fired by the music of Claude Debussy and realising all the commercial possibilities of such a master, came to see our very pleasant Mr. Wholesale at our studios, 118 rue Réaumur.

"Buon giorno! Signori!" it exclaimed, borrowing for the occasion the voice of Caruso. And straight away it followed this up by "Reverenzia" in the voice of Marie Delna.

"Do you know," we asked the Gramophone, "why we asked you to come?"

"Non pas, non pas,
   Messieurs les . . . soldats!"

it replied, this time in the voice of a provincial Micaela.

"Well, now listen. We want to know what sort of impression you had from your meeting with Claude Debussy."

The Gramophone quickly exchanged the opera mechanism for the speech mechanism and now took it upon itself to pinch the voice of old Guitry.

"I might as well tell you straight away," it said. "I was extremely shy. In our profession we are all aware of Debussy's opinions of artificial instruments from the barrel-organ to the toy trumpet. Also, he doesn't usually call upon military bands to play his scores, and of course at first sight I seem to be very brassy. So I made it quite clear to my chief that he should

TO LOUIS LALOY

April 14th 1905

You should know how people have deserted me! It is enough to make one sick of everyone called a man. I shan't tell you of all that I have gone through. It's ugly and tragic and ironically reminds one of a novel a concierge might read. Morally I have suffered terribly. Have I some forgotten debt to pay to life? I don't know; but often I've had to smile so that no one should see that I was going to weep. So, my dear friend, be assured of my joy on seeing you again. I shall try to bring up the old Claude Debussy you knew. If he is rather care-ridden don't mind, for his affection for you is unshaken.

TO LOUIS LALOY

August 28th 1905

It would have been unpardonable to leave Paris without seeing you if my departure had not been a flight. I fled from all that tedious fuss. I fled from myself, who was finally only allowed to think by permission of the usher. I've been here a month. It's a little English seaside place, silly as these places sometimes are. I shall have to go because there are too many

---

pronounce my name, Gramophone, properly, for if Debussy thought he was going to hear the Saxophone we should never hear the end of it.

"Well, there he was. 'Good morning,' he said. He wasn't talking to me, but after all I'm not so sensitive; I'm only concerned about technical improvements. He put his hat on the piano stool and his walking-stick next to it which promptly rolled on the floor. He's a fine-looking man. You see straight away that he is a man of great genius. He looked at me scowling. I daresay I look top-heavy on my little feet, but that is how I am supposed to look. When he finished staring at me he was most polite.

"What more can I say of him? Claude Debussy seems to me, as to all who have heard him, a marvellous composer. Moreover the gramophone is assured by means of his music of an immortality that is both complete and faithful in every way, and he is therefore indispensable."

We took leave whilst the celebrated instrument sang with the voice of Jean de Reszke the aria from *Les Pêcheurs de perles:*

"Je crois . . . l'entendre encore. . . ."

draughts and too much music—but I don't quite know where.
. . . I am trying somehow to get back to myself. I have
written a certain amount of music which I have not done for
quite a time.

TO RAOUL BARDAC

February 25th 1906

My dear Rara,

Forgive my laziness! Well, "regonflons des souvenirs
d'hiver", as Willy would make Mallarmé's Faun say. And what
a winter! Rain, the trees look like disconsolate widowers, and
for a change they've put the flowers inside and the poultry
outside. Vainglorious people try to fill the void with symphonic
descriptions. Well, we heard *Schéhérazade* again. It doesn't
improve with age. It reminds one more of a bazaar than of the
Orient. And of course Chevillard isn't a bit like the princess.
. . . We heard too *Un jour d'été à la montagne* by Vincent
d'Indy. This kind of d'Indy is from beyond the Cévennes. As I
am not very well informed on this place, I can hardly speak of
it. There seemed to be an immoderate use of the bassoon—
and fancy having a piano. I thought they had pianos only in
the mountains of Switzerland.

You didn't have any luck at the Société X. . . . But you
have no reason to feel very resentful. First of all you weren't
properly backed, and then you don't belong to any of the
groups who are allowed to mess things up. You have time to
prepare your play—so don't strike out on a bad line or one
that might lead to nothing.

You are talented, but you can never be too aware of the long
road ahead. You know how little respect I have for the parasite
development which has too long bolstered up the glory of the
Masters. With such a feeling there comes a keener sense of
values and one may discover a melodic line more sensitive to
design and timbre. Let your ideas breathe, for they can so
easily succumb to the pretentiousness of form.

In a word, have patience! It is a major and even a domestic virtue which helps a great deal. But I don't want to spoil a fine day for you with this shower of moral and æsthetic considerations. What's the good? Aesthetics have really only a relative value and I'm afraid that morals have too.

The description of your days is delightful. You are right! It is better to let one's mind soak in the sun—like the flowers and the photographs—while one's nerves can still react.

Gather impressions. But don't hurry to note them down; for music has this over painting, that it can bring together all manner of variations of colour and light. It is a point that is not often observed though it is quite obvious.

And then, from time to time forget music altogether. "Practice makes perfect" is a schoolmaster's notion. And it is not in very good taste to badger those one loves the most with constant requests.

Your mother has a wonderful cold. You know how opposed she is to all medicine, and that doesn't help matters.

Little Chouchou is going to have yet another nurse. The one she has at present says that her husband has been unfaithful to her. So she is going to find out the trouble for herself, which is not very wise and certainly not very economical.

I shan't speak to you of what I am doing. Although I have been writing very little, music offends my ear. The reason for that, we will say, is the colour of the sky.

TO G. JEAN-AUBRY
March 25th 1910

My brother is very likeable but his tastes run to music-halls. I don't blame him! You might have upset him a little in introducing him to music in which there are suggestions of smiles but which does not exactly provoke loud guffaws of laughter. Let us hope that he won't think too badly of us.

What you ask me about Mallarmé's impressions of the music of the *Prélude a l'après-midi d'un faune* goes back a long way.

I used to live then in a little furnished flat in the rue de Lon-
dres. The wallpaper, for some curious reason, represented a
portrait of Monsieur Carnot surrounded by little birds. You
can't imagine the state of mind it brought me to! I simply
could never stay at home.

Mallarmé came in with his prophetic air and his Scotch plaid
around him. After listening to it he remained silent for a long
time; then said: "I didn't expect anything like that. This music
draws out the emotion of my poem and gives it a warmer
background than colour." And here are the lines that Mallarmé
wrote on a copy of *L'Après-midi d'un faune* which he sent me
after the first performance:

> Sylvain d'haleine première,
>   Si ta flute a réussi
> Ouïs toute la lumière
>   Qu'y soufflera Debussy.

Here for anyone who wants it is a first-rate historical document. Anyhow those are my pleasantest memories of a period
when I wasn't yet badgered and bothered with "Debussysme".

TO HENRY RUSSELL

October 5th 1910

My dear Mr. Russell,

You may well have reason to lose patience with me but I
should never have thought you would have treated me in such
an off-hand way. Of course I admit that you have a perfect
right to present my draft to the bank. But do you imagine that
money will just come in this way? It certainly will not and
I'm afraid the only person who will make anything out of it
will be the bailiff.

I wouldn't wish these last few months that I've spent on
anyone. My mother has been ill, my wife too, and I have gone
about with a millstone round my neck. I am not telling you all
this to move you; I am merely stating facts which make it

utterly impossible for me to meet these responsibilities. Before deciding on what you intend to do, do you not think that there might not be another way of going about it? Could this draft not be paid in several instalments? I give you my word of honour that I shall never have the sum of 5,000 francs to pay all at once. Now that the season has begun my hope is that with some new works to be performed funds will be forthcoming to enable me to settle my debts.

You have too often given me proof of your friendship to treat me suddenly as if I were nothing but a common creditor. Help me now, once again, and I assure you that I shall find the means of expressing my gratitude.

If you wish to come and see me, call in the morning, about 10.30 (except tomorrow) when I am more likely to be alone, and continue to believe in my friendly and cordial thoughts for you.

TO ANDRÉ CAPLET

December 22nd 1911

My good Caplet,

I understand your not having replied to my confused letter written in a fit of the blues, but not to have replied to poor Saint Sebastian—this is hardly worthy of you. Sebastian may be used to being struck by arrows, but he doesn't really expect to receive them from you.

But don't let us magnify things. I know that your life of "hard labour" [in English in the original] is calculated to deaden any kind of sensitive feelings; and you can imagine that I haven't breathed a word to anyone regarding the matter of how upset I was at having to abandon my journey to America. I have first of all had in mind my friendship for you built up as a result of a thousand delights we have shared, hardly without our realising them; and I have been thinking that your forthcoming performance of *Pelléas* is likely to be a very rare experience for me. In all this I am something like a child who has been shown

a lovely cake but which he is not allowed to eat. It may be
character-forming but I'm a little old for that. The plain fact
is that I was hurt. But let us say no more about it.

Music does not appear to be much of a support to me either.
I haven't yet managed to finish the two little operas of Poe,
everything strikes me as being so deadly dull. For a single bar
that I write that may be free and alive, there are twenty stifled
by the weight of what is known as tradition, the influence of
which I consider to be hypocritical and despicable. Observe,
if you please, that I am little concerned about the fact that it
may be my own tradition we are talking about. It is nevertheless misleading, for you merely see yourself in different guises.
One must put aside everything that encroaches on one's
thoughts and concentrate very carefully on oneself alone.
What happens, of course, is just the opposite; there is in the
first place the family to reckon with which stands in the way
either through kindness or because they simply do not see
things as they are. And then there are the Mistress temptations,
the Mistress temptation I should say, which one hasn't even
reckoned with, for if only one can forget. . . . And even now
I haven't told you the half. There is nothing one can do about
it: our souls are inherited from a mass of unknown people who
seem from afar to exercise a strange influence on our actions.

I read that you conducted a magnificent performance of
Samson et Dalila. You are capable of everything, even of
bringing back to life a stuffed crocodile. For my sins I heard
La Mer conducted by Gabriel Pierné, it was frightful and em-
barrassing. The same *La Mer* conducted by Camille Chevillard,
much better. As a result of these performances Jacques Durand
and I have decided not to give *Gigues* this year. We shall wait
till next spring when Durand is due to organise another series
of orchestral concerts. May we hope that André Caplet will
offer us his services? In which case the above-mentioned
Gigues will be conducted by him. Announce this, if you like, as
a piece of good news.

Chouchou is still a good little girl who hasn't forgotten her friend Caplet. She speaks about him to people who have never even heard of this illustrious Capellmeister from which she concludes that they must belong to some race of Red Indians.

Satie still hasn't found an odd ten minutes in which to go to America, but he often speaks of you and maintains that a true Norman can never really get on with the Americans and that you will soon give up this idea of yours of believing that you are bound to spend six months of the year over there. I entirely agree with him. Would you not be free around Christmas to spend the New Year with us? Really Boston is a bit too far off the map! . . .

TO CLAUDE-EMMA (CHOUCHOU) DEBUSSY
St. Petersburg, December 11th 1913

My dear little Chouchou,

Your poor father has taken quite some time to answer your dear little letter. But you mustn't be cross with him. He is very sad at the thought of not having seen his pretty little Chouchou for so long, not to have heard her songs and her laughter and to have missed all that noisy fuss which sometimes makes you such an aggravating little thing but more often my own darling.

How is Monsieur Czerny getting on—the composer of such genius? You know that tune of his written for a ballet of fleas?

And old Xantus? Is he still behaving himself? And is he spoiling the garden again? I give you my permission to scold him roundly.

At the Koussevitzky's at Moscow there were two charming

bulldogs who have eyes like the frog in the drawing-room—
we got on very well; I'm sure you would have liked them—and
a bird that sang almost as well as Miss Teyte.

All this was very pleasant, but don't think I could possibly
forget you for a moment: my only thought is to be with you
again. And so think kindly of your dear father and take his
many tender kisses.

Try and look after your dear mother and see that she is not
too unhappy.

TO JACQUES DURAND

August 8th 1914

My dear Jacques,

Your letter has reassured me and I am really glad to have got
your news.

You know that I have no *sang-froid* and certainly nothing of
the army spirit. I've never had a rifle in my hands. My recollections of 1870 and the anxiety of my wife, whose son and
son-in-law are in the army, prevent me from becoming very
enthusiastic.

All this makes my life intense and troubled. I am just a poor
little atom crushed in this terrible cataclysm. What I am doing
seems so wretchedly small. I've got to the state of envying
Satie who, as a corporal, is really going to defend Paris.

And so, my dear Jacques, if you have any work that you can
give me, do not forget me. Forgive me for counting on you,
but you are really all I have.

June 8th 1916

The sick man again thanks you for your friendly inquiries.
As the days go by I must admit that I am losing patience. I have
been tried too long. I wonder whether this illness isn't in-
curable? I might as well be told at once. *Alors! Oh! Alors!* as
poor Golaud cries.

Life has become too hard, and Claude Debussy, writing no

Ravel [1911] by Achille Ouvré

Fauré [1896] Drawing by John Sargent

more music, has no longer any reason to exist. I have no
hobbies. They never taught me anything but music. That
wouldn't matter if I wrote a great deal; but to tap on an empty
head is disrespectful.

October 16th 1916

Le Moulleau has not been able to help me and I shall not
bring back any masterpieces. I might have a few sketches to
be used later. I have never found hotel life so unpleasant. Even
the walls are hostile—not to speak of this life in a numbered
box.

Yesterday I had a visit from X. He made me sorry for a
moment that I had ever written a sonata and made me doubtful
of my own writing. Well, no doubt, there are bad musicians
everywhere. But this incident very much disturbed me. It
means a great deal, and I shall no longer be surprised at the lack
of understanding my poor music meets with. . . . It was
frightening. Why wasn't I taught to polish eye-glasses, like
Spinoza? I should never have expected to earn my living by
music.

TO PAUL-JEAN TOULET

June 20th 1917

Like poor Mélisande, *Je ne fais pas ce que je veux*, which is
indeed the greatest punishment. You imagine Gémier to be
too much of a disciple of Shakespeare. If only you knew the
translation of *The Merchant of Venice* you would be reassured.
All Gémier wants is to use his gifts as a producer and to make
his crowds move about. *As You Like It* will not be of much use
to him for this. But he'll find some means of doing what he
wants, you may be sure. If necessary he'll make the theatre
attendants act or have the people in the stalls go and change
places with the people in the balcony. But without any point-
less jokes, I believe you could do *As You Like It*.

You have never shown me any of your old work and I hold

I

your writing in too great respect to have forgotten it. You couldn't, I imagine, have lost it.

The vocal sections could play a great part in *As You Like It*. I don't want to miss any of the songs that so naturally spring out of the play. I should like you, by the way, to look out for them and to use your lyrical gifts on them.

TO JACQUES DURAND

July 22nd 1917

Up till now I've been horribly tired. My last illness has left me with an aversion to doing anything. There are mornings when dressing is like one of the twelve labours of Hercules and I don't know what I expect—a revolution or an earthquake— so that I shan't have to go on. But without being unduly pessimistic, mine is a hard life. I have to fight against illness and against myself. I feel a nuisance to everyone. . . .

MAURICE RAVEL,
[1875-1937]
GABRIEL FAURÉ
[1845-1924]
ERIK SATIE
[1866-1925]

RESEARCH into the day-to-day life of Maurice Ravel has not so far yielded material significant enough to warrant anything more than an anecdotal biography. In France, apart from the studies of Roland Manuel, Hélène Jourdan-Morhange and Vladimire Jankélévitch, admirable in regard to Ravel's work but necessarily limited on the biographical plane, there has been no serious attempt to uncover the less apparent features of his character. There is a good reason for this. The emotional life of Ravel remains completely inscrutable. The nature of emotional attachments, greatly prized by biographers who have made use of modern psychology, is an important but not the only key to an understanding of behaviour; and it may well be that the picture some future biographer may give us of Ravel will have to be based on a recognition of the fact that the inspiration of a feminine relationship was unknown to him. The one central figure in the composer's emotional life appears to have been his mother; all other relationships, with men as with women, were courteous, amiable but strangely distant. He gave himself to no one.

This fact alone sets the remote figure of Ravel on quite a different plane from the altogether differently remote figure of Debussy. The two composers, once considered almost indentical or at any rate complementary, are now seen to have been curiously opposed. The music of Debussy strikes a very serious blow at tonality; he went far into a world of disintegration—le délicieux mal de l'idée à choisir entre toutes; the art of Ravel, for all the wonder of its detail—here Mozart was one of his ancestors—is never adventurous in this way.

It sounds to us today like some twentieth-century offspring of Mozart and Liszt.

In his day Ravel was unjustifiably accused of preciosity. In his letter to the critic and historian Jean Marnold the composer of L'Heure Espagnole *and* Daphnis and Chloe *condemns this precious interpretation of his music: "Delicate, refined quintessential. . . . Rats! I couldn't believe this was the impression I was making." This letter, like all of the others in this selection, is taken from the illuminating publication* Ravel au Miroir de ses Lettres *by Marcelle Gérar and Rene Chalupt. Ravel was not a voluminous writer. The tone of his letters is frequently dry and business-like, sometimes playful and ironic, but on the whole unexpectedly unsophisticated. From an early journey along the Rhine the pictorial stylist retains an impression not of the Rhine's Romantic associations, but of a manufacturing town with its "smelting castles, incandescent cathedrals and the wonderful symphony of travelling belts, whistles and terrific hammerblows." He gives tiny sketches of his native Basque country, the "fireworks" that amused him at the front during the* 1914 *war, the Orient of his imagination, and we see too that curious trait of his in seeking out fake curios and antiques. He is said always to have prized reproductions above the genuine thing.*

At the thought of leaving his mother at the beginning of the war he is driven to work "with the precision of a madman". This was not just a figure of speech. The mental collapse of Ravel—already perhaps foreseen in the series of empty letters merely giving dates, numbers and times, written during his American tour—must have come about because he was finding the tension of his now unfulfilled emotional life unbearable.

The chaste music of Gabriel Fauré was also highly stylised. Time has not greatly added to the stature of this disciple of Saint-Saëns who laudably places the welfare of his devoted family above his own musical pursuits. Fauré's music can still be balm to us today—for the reason that it was written with a complex absence of any kind of undercurrent of anxiety. Its positive quality is a most attractive blandness. Consider this as an example of Fauréan gentleness:

*"How often I simply cannot say where I am or where I am going!
And how often I have wondered what music is for! What is it?
And what am I trying to express? What are my feelings? What are
my ideas? How can I express that of which I am not aware myself?"*
Nowhere in these simple and often moving letters, all of them addressed to his patient wife, does Fauré rise above this note. He is
absent from his teaching and his organ at the Madeleine for long
periods, working methodically in country hotels; and his almost daily
letters sent to Paris (published as the Lettres Intimes, edited by his
son) thus form a continuous journal. On his journeys to Germany,
Italy, Switzerland and England he responds to some of the novel
surroundings, but apart from an occasional discreet comment on the
moonlight on Lake Lugano or an impenetrable London fog, one
would hardly know that he had gone to one place or another.
Wherever he was, in fact he was all the time in his own private and
industrious world. This was not only because of his natural reserve; he
was cruelly afflicted with a form of deafness which distorted every
musical sound and which made it impossible for him to hear any of his
later works. Fauré bore this appalling punishment without the slightest
trace of bitterness. At the end, in his eightieth year, he writes an unfor-
gettable letter to his faithful wife informing her, in all humility, that
she may have reason to be proud of what he will soon leave behind.

The chasteness of Erik Satie was of another order. Though not a
familiar figure in the Paris musical world until he had reached middle
age, he remained the child among the great. His letters, many of
which have been kindly communicated to me by his friend Valentine
Hugo, alternate between expressions of hopelessness and impotence
on the one hand, and on the other, some kind of pert, unnaturally
buoyed-up confidence. The more familiar view of Satie is of an
exhibitionist and an eccentric.

Are the quirks of Satie as amusing as they seemed to be in his day?
Hardly. Many great names have been associated with him, among
them Moussorgsky and the Douanier Rousseau. But the ideal of a
child-like innocence which they achieved was only partly realised by
Satie. A small number of his works have still this innocent freshness;

others are dated or forgotten. It is clear from this handful of letters and other documents, that when his spontaneous vein failed him eccentricity was the screen he used to conceal impotence. To be sure, many of his contemporaries divined something quite unexpectedly pure in the soul of Satie—"this sweet medieval musician" as he seemed to Debussy "who has strayed into our century by mistake". And tragic it is that what we should now diagnose as a severe neurosis eventually overcame this associate of Picasso, Stravinsky, Debussy and Ravel and left him in the end a pauper at the mercy of his successful friends.

RAVEL

TO MAURICE DELAGE

On board the Aimée

Amsterdam, June 29th 1905

In dry dock in the harbour. We're caulking the bridge and I really don't know what we've got for our future passage. We've been here three days and I have still not been to the museum. There are so many things to see. Amsterdam is quite different from what I imagined. A pile of houses all in different colours and with wrought gables, palaces and modern monuments strange in both colour and architecture. Canals everywhere. The whole town is built on piles and it has a wonderful character but also a foul stench. As soon as I got here I made for the zoo and the aquarium. I think I am going to spend quite some time there.

Excursion yesterday to Alkmaar. A cheese market where there was an eternal ringing of a carillon. On the way, a most magnificent sight. A lake with windmills all round the sides. In the fields the windmills stretch to the horizon. Wherever you look you see sails turning. You begin to feel like an automaton yourself at the sight of this mechanical landscape.

I needn't tell you that I haven't done a stroke of work. But I'm storing my ideas up and I think this trip will yield quite a lot. Anyhow I am perfectly happy for the moment and it was quite wrong of me to worry when for a moment I was stagnating. You know how I magnify things—and there is always something worse! Write to me at Amsterdam. We shall be here for about another week.

Rhine nr. Dusseldorf, July 5th 1905

My dear friend,

Since yesterday we have been in Germany, on the German Rhine. It is not exactly the Rhine I had imagined with legendary associations of nixies, gnomes and valkyries, towns perched on rocks surrounded by pinewoods, Hugo, Wagner and Gustave Doré. It's something like this a little further on, near Cologne apparently. For the moment it's quite good, perhaps even better. What I saw yesterday will remain imprinted on my memory together with the port of Antwerp.

After a muddy journey yesterday along the very wide stretch of river with hopelessly flat and uninteresting banks either side we have come upon a town of chimneys, their roofs spitting rusty brown or blue rockets of flames. This is Haum, a gigantic foundry in which 24,000 men work day and night. Since Ruhrort was too far we are putting in here. And a good thing too, or we should not have seen this wonderful sight. Towards evening we went down to see the factories. How can I tell you about these great smelting castles, these incandescent cathedrals and the wonderful symphony of travelling belts, whistles and terrific hammerblows in which you are submerged? And everywhere the sky is a scorching deep red. On top of it all a storm broke. We came back thoroughly drenched through in rather different moods. Ida who was terrified wanted to cry, and so did I—but from joy. How much music there is in all this!—and I certainly intend to use it.

When we left this morning it was raining. High, very high in the sky, the pale sun shone out. All the time huge blue masses emerged through the yellow mist. And suddenly you see what looks like great fairy palaces—these gigantic factories are to be seen everywhere.

Now the countryside is beginning to look more peaceful. The banks are flat again with little forests here and there. We expect to put up at Dusseldorf tonight.

Write to me at Frankfurt, it will be safer. We expect to stay there five or six days.

TO MME IDA GODEBSKA

August 9th 1905

My dear friend,

Your card was waiting for me when I got back to Paris again. I had been for a few days to Mary-sur-Marne. This time we spent all the time boating, rowing, sculling and sailing. I longed for the water. But now unfortunately I am back on land again and almost quite alone. . . .

About this mission abroad. I'm still worried. . . . I learnt that it was Gaveau, attaché at the Ministry of Fine Arts, who had this wonderful idea . . . and I couldn't help telling him that I wanted to go to the Orient. . . .

I imagined that I was writing letters and going into raptures about the strange surroundings, the crowds of Oriental peoples, the palaces, elephants, monkeys and gazelles; Ceylon too and Batavia. Confound it all! I soon let my imagination run away with me. Last night I dreamt that I was coming out of the station at Constantinople and walking on to a terrace overlooking the Bosphorus. And just as I was about to see some wonderful place they were telling me about, someone came in to wake me up. I grunted a bit and wanted to go back to sleep but I couldn't. So that's as far as I have got. What I should like is formal notice to leave on the spot. Let's have autocracy! . . .

TO JEAN MARNOLD

February 7th 1906

My dear Marnold,

I have been wanting to thank you for some days and have been expecting to see you. And I must now tell you immediately how much your article cheers me up after the one in *Le Temps*. It's not because of your praise (though that counts for a little) but because you understand more what I'm about. Delicate, refined, quintessential. . . . Rats! I couldn't believe that this was the kind of impression I was making.

You see something else in my recent works and I am grateful. What I am writing now is not very subtle, a big Waltz (yes!) in the form of a homage to the great Strauss, not Richard, the other one, Johann. You know what I feel for these wonderful rhythms and what I think of the exuberance of the dance compared to the Puritanism of the César Franck school. I know what to expect from these neo-Christian adepts but I don't care. . . .

What I have tried to do is rather ambitious—to revive the Italian *opera buffa*. But only in theory. This work is not conceived in the traditional form like its ancestor, its only ancestor, *The Marriage* of Moussorgsky which was a faithful portrayal of the play of Gogol. *L'Heure Espagnole* is a musical comedy. There are no changes in the play of Franc-Nohain apart from a few cuts. Only in the final quintet, by reason of its form and florid vocal writing, is there a suggestion of the normal operatic ensembles. Apart from this quintet, I have written simple straightforward declamation rather than florid song. The French language has its stresses and musical inflections like any other. And I don't see why one shouldn't use these correctly in musical prosody.

The spirit of the work is boldly humorous. The irony in it I have sought to express by means of harmony, rhythm and orchestration and not, as in the operetta, by letting the humour of the words pierce the texture.

I had long been thinking of writing a humorous musical work. The modern orchestra did not seem to me in itself sufficient to bring truly comic effects into relief. When I read Franc-Nohain's *L'Heure Espagnole* I saw that here was the droll libretto I was looking for. Many things in it appealed to me, the contrast of everyday speech with exaggerated flights of fancy, and the fact that the characters were set against such unusual and amusing sounds in the clockmaker's shop. And of course there was much to be done with the attractive rhythms of Spanish folk-music.

TO MADAME GODEBSKA

June 19th 1908

Dear friend,

I haven't told you all about *Pelléas*. The reason is that I was ashamed. You can't imagine what it has become. The orchestra of the Olympia Music Hall would have played more sensitively. Musical clowns would have given a better characterisation. You should hear Périer muttering to the stage props sounds that he wouldn't dare utter to the public. X is a delightful doll. Physically she is more suited to the rôle than Garden and she has a better voice, but she sings the part with a complete lack of understanding.

The others sing right out so that they sometimes manage to be heard above the noise of the orchestra. The complete massacre is really too painful for those who remember it as it was. *Boris* will be butchered in the same way before long and so will everything else given in France. . . .

TO MADAME GODEBSKA

September 18th 1908

Dear Friend,

. . . There was a minor tragedy at La Grayette this afternoon. The children are not awfully fond of their English governess and have begun to let her see it. Simply because they call notes by different names in English, Mimi didn't appear at tea-time. And she couldn't be brought out of her hiding-place even though Jean came to tell her that the donkey had arrived. And so Catherine had to be brought on the scene and she had to go and sing for her in the garden. So I really let her know how angry her mother would be and that the donkey would be sent back immediately. I got nowhere with this so I changed my tactics. I told them how disappointed their homesick mother would be to find such hard-hearted children. Mimi and Jean were not exactly moved by this and I was extremely annoyed, but by the time dinner came I had won my point. Mimi began to speak pidgin English and Jean insisted that his governess should eat up everything he didn't want to finish himself. After dinner no end fun, and the children just good-humouredly began to biff each other about.

The governess took it all in good part and did nothing but run up and down the stairs to be smothered with kisses. Jean put on his best manners, called her "petite Miss", begged her to tell him stories and to play the piano to him before he went to sleep and then to come into his bed with him. I only hope it lasts. I can't put on this act before every meal.

Before going to sleep Mimi told me she found the name "Marie" dark but that "Olga" was light and clear. I find this even better than Rimbaud.

TO MADAME GODEBSKA

Ziburu, July 19th 1911

Dear friend,

Are things beginning to take a turn for the better with you? Are you soon going to be able to get to your wonderful pine-forest? If only you had made up your mind to come here to see the acacia trees running along the seashore! And the soft green hills with little clumps of oak-trees, neatly trimmed as they are in the Basque country, looking as if they are going to roll down. And high above, the Pyrenees mauve as in fairy-land. And then of course there is the light. The sun isn't fierce here as it is in the Mediterranean *midi*; it's delicate in its brightness. And the people are like that too. They are spirited and distinguished, exuberant too but not coarse, light-footed in their dancing but not exaggeratedly sensuous. Even the Church here—and the people are devout—has a streak of scepticism. . . . But I must stop; I must be off to Dombane

Loihilzum (St Jean-de-Luz as they say in France) to see Madame Vicq-Challet. Let me hear from you soon and make an effort to come and see us when you have had enough of the staid prettiness of Brittany.

TO MAURICE DELAGE

August 4th 1914

Mon cher vieux,

Write to me directly you receive this so that I might at least have the feeling of a friend around.

There are all sorts of people here whom I like very well. But that's not what I mean. . . .

If only you knew what I'm going through. All day long, without a moment's respite, the same terrifying obsession: if I had to leave my poor old mother it would surely kill her. And the country is not exactly waiting for me to save it.

But this is all a rationalisation and I can't help feeling that before long my tension will snap. To avoid anything of the sort I just work.

Yes indeed, I'm working with the precision and the lucidity of a madman.

But at the same time something gnaws away at me all the time and all of a sudden I find myself sobbing over my sharps and flats!

Of course when I come down and face my poor mother I must appear to be quite normal and even entertaining. But the point is, can I keep it up?

All this has been going on for four days, since the declaration of war.

Write to me straight away, I beg of you.

TO ROLAND MANUEL

March 17th 1916

My dear friend,

The letter to your mother has just gone and I want to use

the little free time I have while I drink my tea and have the last
of the biscuits. Boredom needs food, and what a hungry thing
boredom is. . . . This is the fourth meal it's driven me to and
I'm no better off.

There you are . . . finding me with nothing to do a corporal has just asked me to help him clear the bridges.

So that's that!

And now they're doling out the soup—I'll write to you
tomorrow.

TO ROLAND MANUEL

March 18*th* 1916

. . . It's quaint but not unpleasant to walk about this little
town, quite attractive in itself—in fact I've only seen it at
night and don't expect to see it at any other time—from which
the nearest point of the front is 30 km. But we are actually very
near the big battle 40 km away. (I now understand very well
how awkward people feel in the normal surroundings of
Paris). Crowds of soldiers with a few civilians in between mill
around in the darkness with a streak of light here and there from
a half-open door, drapers' shops and sugared almonds and
preserves in the shop windows all brightly lit up. And there
are incessant convoys of truck-loads of men going off to the
battle. At each turning, a big illuminated sign with a name on it
and an arrow. Almost every evening first the factory siren and
then the station siren goes off when the Zeppelins come. When
we are directly threatened they sound the "Take cover"
warning. Whereupon all the civilians come out and poke their
noses in the air.

Good Lord! I'm on duty now, I must hurry. . . .

TO MADAME FERNAND DREYFUS

April 15th 1916

I'm in the blues again, dear *marraine*. I put it down to a
bit of everything, the weather, my transfer and the lack of
sleep.

I told you, I think, that I was very well off thanks to the
chief of the depot, Lieutenant Bloch, who on the advice of a
friend of mine, a captain, took a very kindly attitude to an
inexperienced soldier like me. But then Wednesday last this
lieutenant left. And things soon changed: quite naturally, in
the army, as in fact it would have happened in civilian life too,
I was just chucked out of my job. On Wednesday I drove about
from seven in the morning to eight o'clock at night in drench-
ing rain. I was soaked through and I could wring my clothes
out. Next day I was told I was to be sent to X quite near the
front. We have quite nice quarters in a castle—in the barn of
course—but we've got beds without any unpleasant smells,
fresh air and lovely grounds. Before we go to bed we watch
the fireworks. The cannon-fire rocks us to sleep and also some
devil of an engine that lights up the battle scene. Day duty is
not too bad but the awful thing is that there is often night
duty. Every three or four days we drivers have to act as
stretcher-bearers. I let it be known that I feared I was really not
strong enough for these duties. And so I was put on to this
engine. It's not so wearing but I'm on duty more often, at
least every other day. So I wonder whether I shall be able to
put up with this lack of sleep and drive properly during the
day. Also I am beginning to feel farther and farther away. I
haven't had any news now for three days.

I received your nice letter just as I was leaving and I read it
on the way. Thank you and thank you again for looking after
my dear mother. With all my trouble that's all I am thinking
about. I've told her how I'm placed. I even told her we were
quite near the front, so that she shouldn't think I was hiding

anything, but I didn't let her think there was anything dangerous.

TO MADAME FERNAND DREYFUS

February 9th 1917

I am writing to you in my landlady's kitchen. It's really too cold in my room. . . . I am still all right physically, though I don't imagine for long. Food not exactly ideal: potatoes the only vegetable. But mentally I'm in a frightful state. It seems only yesterday that I was writing to her [Ravel's mother] or that I received one of her dear letters, and how happy I was. There was something foreboding in the background, still I was all right. I didn't imagine it would come so quickly. Now I am in a state of terrifying despair and anxiety. I don't think it is good for me to be away from dear Edward [Ravel's brother]. My captain says I must shake myself out of it. He has made me second-in-command of a car and is going to have me go to the front. I don't think it will make much difference. I am more than ever grateful to you for not having left me alone. I am among jolly friends but I feel more alone here than anywhere. . . .

TO ROLAND MANUEL

May 15th 1923

May I ask you to be good enough to call at an antique dealer's in the rue de Bourgogne and to collect an old-fashioned tobacco-jar and a Greco-Roman watch-stand that I got there yesterday. . . .

TO EDOUARD RAVEL

On the way to Minneapolis, February 21st 1928

Was at Denver yesterday. Spent a good night. Went to bed at 9. We soon arrive at Ohama where we change trains. Leave tonight at 10 after hearing the famous Ohama jazz. The altitude

Fauré [1898] by John Sargent

Satie [1920] Drawing by Pablo Picasso

of Denver where I spent three days is about 5000 feet (gold and silver mines). Wonderful air. Glorious sunshine. It looks a bit overcast. I'm afraid it's going to be cold in New York next week.

Loving thoughts for you all.

K

FAURÉ

TO MADAME FAURÉ

Bayreuth, August 6th 1896

When you get this letter I don't think you'll remember the last one you sent me: you imagine I am going to be greatly stimulated by this whole atmosphere here that is steeped in Wagner. Not at all! My feeling is that we are all getting more and more stupid. All we can speak about are the performances, and there is not one of us who can really put into words what he feels. We are absolutely overcome by all these wonderful things and all our discussions—and we have very many—come to nothing. It's rather like *The Ring* itself in fact, which is built on a philosophy and all sorts of symbolical ideas which ultimately reveal nothing but our hopeless misery and impotence. When it is over you are made more aware than ever of the external values of despair and grief and that's about all. Not very amusing in fact. In a word, the work amounts to the most noble form of repentance, it is almost a kind of contrition.

Dear Marie, I feel what I want to say but I somehow can't find the words. If it were not for the fact that many people would be deprived of great things I should like to see performances of Wagner forbidden anywhere but at Bayreuth. You must really forget the daily routine of life and become here one of the faithful to do justice to the drama of *The Ring*, for in many a place, if the meaning of the action on the stage is not appreciated, the music is unintelligible or seems to be needlessly drawn out. These gods and goddesses have some very extraordinary lessons for us and the fairy tale of *The Ring* has some very strange and unbelievably sad secrets. But it's very, very tiring. Every evening after the performance I feel as if I had walked from the Madeleine to the Bastille and back ten times over. I wish you were with me here. You'd be impressed by it too. And in a good way. Fortunately there is also the quiet of the beautiful country, the silent trees and the wide horizons. . .

Bayreuth, August 8th 1896

Today some people are coming from Bayreuth to play one of my quartets (the second) and my sonata. Risler will play the piano, Friedrich, quite a good violinist from Paris and two instrumentalists from the Bayreuth orchestra will play the other parts.

The fourth performance of the entire *Ring* which I'm going to hear again begins tomorrow and ends Wednesday. So I hope to leave Thursday. I am absolutely permeated with *The Ring*, it haunts me day and night. I don't think these works are models or that it would be possible to copy them. But they inspire you to all sorts of ideas. I am absorbed by them in the way that water seeps through sand.

August 9th 1896

. . . Yesterday evening there was a reception at Madame Wagner's. A curious mixture of people, some of them interesting but others as stupid as could be. They served everything to eat imaginable, even cold leg of lamb. It was all very German and formal, stiff and unsophisticated. But it was worth going to—for once. The daughters of Mme Wagner are pleasant and unaffected. Their mother, with all her affected courtesies, is less genuine.

Today we are going to be submerged again in Wagner's epic music. I find that I am perpetually tired and yet we really do not exert ourselves. The weather is oppressive and damp. Despite the beauty of the scenery, I prefer our Parisian atmosphere and our Parisian friends with all their faults. The fact is that they have no eye here for visual pleasure. Everything is pretentious and gross. Their only values are those of the mind and of discipline.

Yes, I am happier in Paris, but when actually I am in Paris I'd rather be anywhere in the world. Oh senseless man that I am—poor little atom, as you say! But when we are together, you and our children, we have at any rate between us affection and love. This is all that matters together with a few books, a few pieces of sculpture, certain pictures and the music of a few rare people.

Lausanne, August 11th 1903

I am doing everything I can for my health in the hope of improving my hearing. I am constantly aware how little music I am really able to hear and this fills me with an ever-increasing sadness. There is no doubt that over the last year I have got very much worse.

Lausanne, August 12th 1903

I am horror-stricken by this trouble with just that faculty that I prize most highly. It would be disrespectful or at any rate immodest on my part to compare myself with Beethoven. But the latter part of his life was in fact nothing but a long agony. The truth is that there are certain phrases of music, certain combinations of sounds of which I hear nothing, absolutely nothing at all, whether it is my own music or not. This morning I laid out some music paper on the table in the hope of being able to work. But there descended upon me a frightful shroud of misery and discouragement.

Lausanne, August 15th 1903

The rain today has helped me to be able to work. The country is all the same very beautiful; it was oppressive yesterday but it is now very pleasant and fresh and the smell of the earth and the wet leaves is delightful. In Paris I should have had two enormous Masses to perform and those endless vespers. Yet I am sorry not to be with you, except in my thoughts and my heart on this day of embraces and when you will be pressing bouquets of flowers on each other. [The occasion was the joint birthdays of Mme Fauré and her mother.]

Lausanne, August 28th 1903

This morning I worked well but I came up against a wall. there was a knot that I couldn't undo. I shall have to wait until tomorrow. . . .

August 29th 1903

How often I simply cannot say where I am or where I am hoping to go. And how often I have wondered what music is for. What is it? And what am I trying to express? What are my feelings? What are my ideas? How can I express that of which I am not aware myself?

September 1st 1903

The knot in my music is still with me. But I have hopes of seeing my way through. . . . I don't know whether I am merely imagining this but I think that I am beginning to hear music less imperfectly. I have had less trouble with my piano over the last ten days or so. I haven't heard those double sounds which are excruciating. I thought I should go mad!

September 2nd 1903

I have been working here all the morning and hope now to conclude my work satisfactorily. . . . Yesterday I couldn't settle down very well and so I went to Nay which my grandparents had spoken to me about. Came back late but slept very well. The sunsets these last three evenings and the moon rising have been so beautiful I could have wept. . . .

Zurich, August 20th 1904

Slept very badly last night, for no particular reason. But in the snatches of sleep I dreamt of Saint Saëns and this morning I read in *Le Figaro* an article by him on the use of the silent *e*. I also dreamt of the Abbé Pa and in the same copy of *Le Figaro* there was his name. Curious instances of telepathy. In my dream I also heard a work of Gounod and another of Schumann, both of them quite unknown and which were absolutely pure Gounod and pure Schumann.

August 21st 1904

I should love to find here, and I might well do so, a few kindly fiddlers to try out what I've written. There are plenty of musicians here. Unfortunately they are Germans through and through and accordingly distrustful, not to say contemptuous, of French music directly it is anything but superficially gay, amusing or sentimental. You have only to travel a little to be struck by the conceit of people for their own achievements. We are supposed to have a certain chic and high spirits— nothing more!

August 27th 1904

A good day yesterday. The weather was milder and the sky brighter, disclosing in the distance the snow-capped mountains. It is always lovely to see the play of sunlight on rocks, water, trees and fields. What varieties of colour, what brilliance and softness! I wish my music could reflect as much. I am constantly aware of the fact that I do not seem to find anything strikingly different from the music I have already written. Which proves that I am not unduly proud of what I am doing. No matter; the main thing is that what I'm doing must go on.

August 31st 1904

Getting on very well, but sleep poorly though I work a little every evening so as not to go to bed too early. From the terrace I see the lights of the myriad street lamps of Zurich but the moon persists in rising from behind and I do not see it.

Worked yesterday from half-past one to half-past six without stopping. Then took a walk through the apple orchards and fields until a quarter to eight and worked again after dinner until half-past eleven. Heard for the first time midnight strike from all the great clocks of the town.

This is what I have done: the first movement [of the 1st Quintet] has been completely reworked and brought to its climax. But I want it to be striking, and that is what I am trying to achieve at the moment. This first movement is long. I'm half way through the *Adagio*. I hope to get down to it in three or four days. I have a good idea too of the two other movements. But this going over and adjustment of my work has been very difficult. And now that I read it over and listen to it in my head its naturalness strikes me as very, very unreal.

September 18*th* 1904

Last night I worked until half-past twelve. True, up till five o'clock I hadn't made any progress at all. But I did eventually find what I was looking for when I went to have tea in a very fashionable restaurant which I came across yesterday on the edge of a pine forest. I had know about it but I didn't realise what it was. I am constantly coming across beautiful places like this just at the hour of sunset which is always the most beautiful moment of the day. And yesterday evening, because I hadn't lowered the blinds, I saw while I was working the lovely reflection of the white moon in the lake. . . .

September 21*st* 1904

Something very amusing has happened to me recently. Whilst I was thinking of a thousand different things of no importance whatever a kind of rhythmical theme in the style of a Spanish dance took shape in my mind. And this theme just went on its own way, so to speak, without bothering me in any way. But the strange thing was that while I was thinking of a thousand other things, this theme developed of itself, became harmonised in many different ways, changed and underwent modulations, in fact it germinated by itself. Obviously, it drew upon the store of my memories ever since I have been in the world—on all those musical textures which have become part of myself. But how strange is this unconscious functioning of the mind, this precise working out of an idea in this way! If I were to write it down it would have a very definite form.

October 3rd 1904

Now this is as far as I've got. Picture a big dog which has at the end of its tail a luttle curly tuft. Well it's this particular tuft that bothers me. If it's still curly by the time I bring it back to Paris no matter. Only I don't want to burn the dog's tail. So you may take the second movement to be finished although I will confess to you that it still needs another ten or twelve bars that I might find on the way, perhaps in the train, or in the tram or anywhere. So you'll have something to sew up and something to cut out. Get ready a big pair of scissors. Yet by tomorrow I may well have written the whole thing.

Cologne, January 10th 1905
Dom Hotel (Eau de Cologne on all floors!)

I was well replenished yesterday in the German fashion: lunch at two, supper at ten after going to the Opera where they played *Norma* which I had never seen before. It is full of melodies which delighted our fathers but which require a technique of singing that is completely lost. The performance was given in a splendid new theatre, very spacious but built and painted in a tremendously heavy and ugly German style.

The town of Cologne is enormous, full of life and very clean. There are many beautiful old churches besides the famous Cathedral which is just across the way. But what a number of statues of Emperors high up on their horses all over the place! I've seen on the banks of the wide and beautiful Rhine the statue of the wretched Frederick. It's gigantic and he is set up there with a commanding gesture as if he were addressing the

entire universe. When you think of his oppressive reign you
have a fair idea of the silliness of humanity.

It is just in this way that they are so tremendously powerful,
these Germans who are so different from ourselves. When you
see how hard and unpolished they are now you wonder what
they must have been like in the fourteenth century. But what
power and order and strength everywhere and in everything.
It's overwhelming!

Frankfort, January 16th 1905

I am longing to be amongst you all again. I am exhausted by
the Germans, amiable as they all wish to be, and I'm really
suffering from musical indigestion. There is no doubt that they
have some splendid qualities; but they have not our perception
nor our reactions. The amusing thing is that what they criticise
in my music is its lack of warmth, its severity! We are certainly
not the same kind of people. Madame de Rothschild has advised me—these are her very words—to come back to Frankfort
with a pretty woman, well dressed, who is able to sing my
"chansons". Then I should be able to make money. For everyone here sings what they call my "chansons".

I've been to see all the monuments of Frankfort and today it
is below freezing point. There is another concert tonight. There
is at least one a day. And they listen to them all in the same
quiet way, just as if they were eating another meal, just as if it
were another daily function of life. . . .

Stresa, August 31st 1906

I look from here on to Pallanza, twenty minutes away by
boat. Stresa is a town of hotels. Around, the countryside still
and quiet. . . . I slept divinely in a room lit up by an enormous
window reaching down to the floor, with a balcony from which
you have a view like fairyland. On my arrival yesterday I
beheld, as the sun peacefully went down, the most beautiful
sight one could ever see. The great mountains, the immense

stretch of the lake and the colours of the water, the islands and
the surrounding country were unbelievably moving. . . .

September 1st 1906

I am more and more impressed by the wonderful panorama
at Stresa, tremendous in size and full of exquisitely coloured
details as in fairyland. The rose-laurels here and the magnolia
trees are enormous. In the hotel garden there is, among many
wonders, a great alley of reeds intertwined in the form of an
extraordinary vault. This garden with its many different
flowering shrubs and all kinds of trees is a paradise tended at
night by gardeners who must surely be angels. You see to
what flights I am inspired. . . .

September 5th 1906

The days here are glorious and the evenings delightful. I
shan't even try to describe the magical reflections of the moon
on the lake. The whole scene is covered in a grey-blue,
silvery softness; the mountains take on an appearance of remote ghosts of gods and goddesses and the boats on the lake
make their way through trails of light like flies in quicksilver.

It is both shady and airy, so that I am able to work in my
room ideally. I was there yesterday the whole afternoon until
half-past six. The verses I am setting [*La Chanson d'Eve*] are
difficult for they are descriptive and not in the least sentimental.
I have to find the music for God The Father and His daughter
Eve, not exactly easy personalities to deal with. . . . I have
certainly lost my heart to the guitar, the mandoline and the
Neapolitan songs. From a distance these sounds are most pleasing as they gently reach the ear and enter into your mind. Not
at all like our stupid and vulgar Parisian songs.

September 7th 1906

Yesterday was a day made out of grey silk, so to speak.
Overcast, very hot and sultry. Everyone went about mopping

himself in complaining mood. Dressed in flannels, I worked seven hours and found ultimately the music to be sung by God. When you see what this eloquence amounts to you may well be surprised that I spent so long over it. But there you are: true simplicity, these days, is the most difficult thing to conceive. . .

September 11th 1906

I was delighted with the very nice letter of Philippe [Fauré's son and biographer]. It was charming and his analysis so much to the point that you might readily believe that the finale [of the A major Sonata] conveys all that he sees in it. I must confess, however, that I thought of nothing of the sort and that in fact I was concerned with no exterior thoughts of any kind. True enough the second theme of the finale is like the cock's crow.

It was only once in the *andante* of my second Quartet that I remember wishing to set down—and even then it was almost unconsciously—the very remote memory of the sound of bells ringing one evening at Montgauzy—you see it was a long time ago—and which came from a village called Cadizac when the west wind blew. The tolling of these bells drew out all sorts of ideas which like all such musings simply could not be put into words. An incident such as this does in fact frequently promote a torpid state of mind, and a very agreeable one, in which thoughts merge imperceptibly into each other. Are we at this moment reaching out to that other world? This is in fact where music begins.

Lausanne, August 16th 1907

After the storm and rain of last night the weather is cooler. It is very pleasant and I am working hard. I'll tell you where I've got to. The music of the spinners [in *Pénélope*] forms a single piece. It opens and is developed and just when it should be brought to an end it is suspended, so to speak, by means of a chord depicting the musings of the damsels, and you then hear a burst of laughter announcing the arrival of the Suitors outside. So I have to deal with a new problem: the servants recount who the Suitors are, what they propose to do, and the resistance to them by the sorrowful Penelope, also the greedy feelings of the Suitors for these easy-going servants. Now all this must be perceived by the audience's ears, the dialogue must be clear and you must know from the music who the characters are. This is the Wagnerian conception; and indeed there is none better. I have already decided on the theme of Penelope. This theme forms the opening material of the Prelude which I have so far left incomplete because I have not yet found the other theme to counter-balance it. This is to be the theme of Ulysses.

As for the Suitors, I have got a theme that characterises them which I am trying out, but it does not yet satisfy me entirely. It is rather Wagnerian. Clearly this devil of a composer foresaw everything. I have been trying to find something to give an impression of brutality and of complete self-satisfaction. And when I say I am trying it out I mean that I am testing its adaptability to various situations. For instance, one of the servants says, of one of the Pretenders: "*Antinoüs est beau*". My theme must at this point spread out its tail like a peacock.

I am also anxious to see whether this theme can be combined with the theme of Penelope. I want to explore every means of changing it, showing it in a different light, either the whole of it or parts of it. It amounts to making a kind of card index of the theme or studies, if you like, as one might make for a painting. This necessary preparation will take me some time but it will enormously facilitate my work later on. You mustn't then worry if I am not able to record my daily progress. It won't mean at all that I am wasting time. What happens is that the mind becomes alive and proceeds from one thing to another. I want to make my effects very clearly, and this worries me somewhat.

Lausanne, August 23rd 1907

Received this morning a word from Paul Dukas, an artist whom I admire enormously in every way, saying that he is on his way. He is coming from Chamonix and Mont Blanc. He is not much of a talker; we shall therefore spend a good day together each thinking of his music.

August 26th 1907

You really must believe what I say in my letters for I mean every word I write. I want them to bring you all the support and goodness that yours bring me. When I was young, Saint-Saëns often used to tell me that I was without a certain defect which, in an artist, is a quality. This was ambition. So I am —— pleased with my work and position at the Conservatoire not just for myself alone. You know how ready I am to talk of my achievements in this field; and you may also remember how as a child I was always, according to my parents, quiet and thoughtful. Therefore it is not only for myself that I am dedicating myself to my present work and that I am trying to arouse that enthusiasm for my work which was never a very strong point of mine; I have you in mind and our children. And constantly I reflect my ideals in you all much more than you might imagine.

Dukas is still here but doesn't distract me in the least. Yesterday I went on working very well up till half-past five. Now I must begin to make studies for the following section. But over the last five days I have forged ahead with my earlier work. The plan of the drama is thus taking better shape every day. But how the days pass!

22 Old Queen St.,
Westminster,
London, March 15th 1908

Here I am being looked after by my "nurse" [i.e. Frank Schuster] who as soon as it was light had a wonderful sirop brought into my room because I had been coughing during the night. The butler is half Burmese, half Chinese and doesn't know a word of French. But what manners! He is all velvet. I arrived in London at five and dined out at eight o'clock at the house of a Member of Parliament of whom I don't even know the name. The dinner and the reception was held "to meet Monsieur Fauré". And there's to be a lunch and dinner on these lines every day of the week.

So much for the esteem in which I am held. The purely commercial aspect of my visit is less impressive. I am told that in regard to the concert on Wednesday the absence of the King, which has caused the whole of the London aristocracy to move to the South of France, will do us a great deal of harm. We must wait and see. At all events I am able to state that my music is well known here and that I am considered a gentleman of importance. . . .

March 21st 1908

Last night I accompanied Madame Raunay in my songs before the Prince and Princess of Wales. The Queen sent her regrets again through our Ambassador at not being able to come to the concert. She spoke to him of me in the most flattering terms and said that she regretted that there was not now time to ask me to play at the Palace but that she would like to know when I was returning to London. I should then be launched in style!

March 22nd 1908

The Queen has asked me to come to the Palace tomorrow for a musical reception.

March 23rd 1908

The reception given by the Queen and the Empress of Russia is over and it was all very friendly. I took along a young American singer who has an American father, a Swiss mother;

she herself was born in Florence and looks like a Japanese girl. But she sings my songs very well and we offered their Majesties the good old things: *Les Berceaux, Le Secret,* the *Sérénade toscane, Après un rêve, Les Roses d'Ispahan* and *Nell.*

There were no guests; only people of the Court. The frightful thing is that the Queen wants to visit our Conservatoire and see how the classes are run. As a matter of fact she is deaf. But she is not blind and will obviously be surprised at our wretched state.

December 2nd 1908

After your white mists of Paris I now have an experience of the frightfully dirty fog of London. It's like the middle of the night. I was afraid of the performance of *Pelléas.* And how surprised, and annoyed, Colonne would be if he were told that this was not the way to play it. . . .

Yesterday at the home of an excellent pianist—an amateur now that she is married—I played my *Ballade* in the two-piano form and my first Quartet (once again!), also for two pianos. This evening at the home of a Member of Parliament where I am dining, there will be no music—at least so they say. To be sure, if they start on European politics I shall be much happier, at any rate for a change.

In dispersing my music throughout the world I think principally of my family and it is for you all that I am hoping to build up my reputation. . . .

December 3rd 1908

It is as if we were in the depth of night and everything is lit up. If a function in life produces its appropriate organ, climate has its effect on behaviour. There can be no doubt that the comforts of English life and their well-appointed houses are a product of this unpleasant climate. And on the musical level these black skies cause people to gather together and to create amateur choirs of an unrivalled standard above anything we know in France. If only our climate weren't so good! Tomorrow evening I shall be dining at the home of Lord Beresford, a high-ranking figure of the British fleet. I imagine they'll serve fried torpedoes!

Lugano, October 1st 1909

I have looked over my work [*Pénélope*] very carefully: I think I have brought out my characters, in both the second and first acts, successfully. I haven't made any particular wilful effort; I have just allowed myself to be led by the simplicity of the action and the dignity of the characters. This was my procedure in *Prométhée*. All the same the impression created at the piano is *terribly cold* and the general feeling stiff and formal. It's only when I listen in my mind to what I have written that I derive some satisfaction. I should really try and trust the opinion of someone else. But who? Just now I am really upset. Perhaps by the time I have let all this rest for two or three weeks I shall begin to see things a little more clearly. The public today is moved only by the complicated but extemely valid polyphony of Wagner, the lights and shades of Debussy or the vulgar emotional wrigglings of Massenet, whilst the frank and open music of Saint-Saëns, to which I am particularly drawn, leaves everyone indifferent. The thought of all this sends a cold shiver down my back, yet if I hadn't these apprehensions I shouldn't be anything of an artist.

Helsingfors, November 14th 1910

The enthusiastic reception I was given yesterday at the Conservatoire [of St. Petersburg] moved me tremendously. What a pity Dubois and Widor weren't there to witness it—no doubt they would have found the enthusiastic welcome I received excessive! . . . Just imagine! A large concert hall decorated with shrubs and flowers. Fanfares of trumpets on my arrival, bouquets presented to me by pretty young ladies, a charming speech made by the Director, a very large gathering

of guests and pupils, a very nice concert of my works, a sump-
tuous buffet and a whole crowd of young people shouting
"Fauré! Fauré!" to bring the walls down! You really cannot
expect enthusiasm of this degree of warmth except in very
cold countries! But jokes apart, it was delightful and I was most
touched. . . . I returned to Petersburg tomorrow night; shall
spend the day with the Zilotis, charming people, and shall be
in Moscow Thursday morning.

Lugano, August 10*th* 1911
The moon moves through the evening air and shines on the
lake in a beautiful mild atmosphere with not a breeze anywhere. But over the last two days I have been up against this
wall again—this terrible wall that I find myself facing now and
again and which is so hard to get through. I have however made
progress in the reconstruction of an entire scene [of *Penelope*]
with which I was not in the least satisfied.

Lugano, August 12*th* 1911
I am happy in this place because apart from the fact that it is
delightful, in regard to material comforts I have never been so
happy anywhere. It is so calm and quiet, not like a hotel at all.
And the owners are the most kind and thoughtful of people. I
have here what I seek beyond everything, space and peace; a
wonderful view and light too and the activities of a pleasing
and very clean little town when I want to go out. I am greatly
pleased to have had the courage to re-write so much of my
music—and there is more to come!

Monte Carlo, April 1*st* 1919
I notice that my hearing is worse in the morning than late
in the day. Unfortunately my appalling hearing is getting worse
every day. I went to hear at the Opera on Saturday an opera of
Verdi of which I had only seen the score a long time ago. All I

L

heard were sounds so wildly distorted that I thought I was going out of my mind. The point is that when a deaf person listens to the spoken word he hears very feebly and indistinctly. But when it comes to music a most extraordinary thing occurs: the intervals between low notes become more and more distorted the lower the music becomes, and correspondingly the same degree of distortion applies to intervals in the higher register. You can imagine what all this leads to. It is diabolical. These were the caricatures of sounds I heard when I listened to *Pénélope*. The human voice is the least painful music for me to listen to. But an instrumental ensemble is nothing but the most painful chaos.

Monte Carlo, April 14th 1919

The atmosphere of this ensemble consisting of my *Madrigal*, *Clair de Lune*, *Pavane* and other pieces [performed in the form of a ballet at the Monte Carlo Theatre], all rather evocative and nostalgic, might easily have been upset by the action on the stage. But it was not and there was very much Verlaine's conception of Watteau:

Jouant du luth et dansant et *quasi*
    Tristes sous leurs déguisements fantasques!

Gunsbourg's production was a bit heavy and showy. Carré would have treated the subject with more subtlety. Anyhow these two performances—there are not to be any others—were very successful. I was pleased to compose and orchestrate the little Overture and the dances. Reynaldo Hahn said that it was like the music of a Mozart who had himself imitated Fauré! An amusing idea and at any rate original. The orchestra here is wonderful and many of the people who listened to it—not me of course—simply lapped it up.

Nice, March 24th 1921

Your letter was calculated only to cause me distress. But you did the right thing in sending it to me. Your character is definite and clear-cut. Mine is not. When I die I shall still be the elusive person that I have always been.

You once reproached me with wanting to score at your expense. My hope has been that as my reputation developed— a matter with which I am personally no longer concerned because it has come too late—you would find some compensation in it for my faults as a man.

You have often reproached me with championing the cause of people who were looked askance at. I have championed them because I didn't believe the things that were said, because I have a fund of naïvety (yes, *na–i–vety*) which has always inclined me to think of the good things rather than the bad. You reproach me for my silence or for being a man of few words. All my life, even as a child, I have been reserved, and have only been able to let myself go on certain occasions.

Grant me at any rate one quality among so many faults: I have never been in the least complaining. Many people might well grumble at seeing themselves, after what is called a fine career, entering upon old age afflicted with terrible infirmities (I have never heard a note of *Pénélope* except in my mind) and also with poverty, for I haven't really a sou of my own!

Nice, April 6th 1922

You spoke to me in one of your last letters of your wonder at the Creation and your poor opinion of humanity. Are you right? The Universe represents order and Man disorder. But is it is his fault? He has been cast on to this earth where everything seems to us to follow some order and from the day of his birth until his death he stumbles through life as best he can. He has been cast on to the earth with his physical and moral burdens (so much so that the theory of original sin had to be invented to explain it all); he goes through life with the mind of a child that wishes to behave itself, however difficult this may be, but only of course if there is a reward at the end. And what is the reward for this child who is man? The knowledge of having thus been perpetually wounded for the future of humanity? Is there one human being out of ten thousand who would accept this? The ultimate proof of our misery is the assurance given to us, the most satisfying assurance of all, of the complete forgetfulness of self, the Nirvâna of the Hindus, or our own *Requiem æternam*.

No, this wretched bundle of evil which is Man, this being condemned to fight for life and whose first and most appalling duty is to devour others before he is devoured himself, deserves more pity than is usually granted him. For years and years I have been wanting to suggest this theory, by no means original, as an alternative to your own extremely bitter conception. There happen to be two dogs here: an old bitch, almost blind, who bumps into every piece of furniture, and also a fine big wolf-hound. When the bitch is fondled while the wolf-hound is about he simply tears off to the white bearskin on the drawing-room floor and tries to bite its ears off. There's Man for you. He is madly jealous but daren't take it out on his master. Do you not agree? And please don't now say that I am unresponsive.

Annecy-le-Vieux, October 14th 1924

I am getting on well, very well, quite as well as when I left Paris. I have abided by all the advice and have felt the benefit of it until I began to feel tired as a result of finishing my Quartet. I have an appetite, I enjoy the lovely sky, everything in fact and I want everyone around me to be happy. So you see I am in no kind of depressed mood.

In my quiet retreat here you can imagine how much I thought of the birthday celebrations of June 14th—those infinitely simple and moving feelings that inspired your dear father. Look around you, please, and look even further afield and tell me if anyone else has been able to find so much joy in life. And if you will allow me to associate myself with your father—and I am sure that you will—tell me where there has been a daughter, and a wife, who has been so proud of the noble works of her father and at the same time of the similarly beautiful and disinterested creations of her husband. Yours has been a sorrowful life and what you have perhaps missed most is not having yourself achieved your ambition. But have you not in yourself a deep satisfaction and the happiness of having brought up your sons in these stormy times, bitter with rivalry —is all this nothing? I hope you will understand what I wish to convey and that you will read these lines for what they are worth. Please do not try to see anything in them nor look for anything in them that is not the simple bare truth.

When I return to Paris I shall systematically sort out all my sketches and notes, everything which I do not want to remain after me, and ask you to burn them all. This was very much on my mind when I was ill. You must help me to see this is carried out. Take care of yourself; I shall be with you on Saturday.

I kiss you from the bottom of my heart.

SATIE

TO CONRAD SATIE

1900(?)

I am overcome with ennui to the extent of dying of a broken heart. Everything I quietly begin to undertake fails in the most spectacular fashion.

I am beginning to turn on God Himself and have got to the state of wondering whether He is not more unfortunate than all powerful.

What news have you? . . . Your future will not be like mine, fortunately for you. You will have a horse, a big carriage, open in summer, closed in winter; and you will go wherever you wish, like the people of leisure.

I take you into my poor arms.

TO CONRAD SATIE

1910

In 1905 I began to work with d'Indy. I was tired of being reproached with an ignorance of which I was aware and which had been noticed in my work by competent authorities.

After three years' heavy work I received my diploma of counterpoint from the Schola Cantorum signed by my excellent master who is the wisest and the best man in this world. Thus in 1908 I was licensed to hold the title of contrapuntist. Proud of my knowledge I began to compose. My first work then was a Choral and Fuge for four hands.

I have been in some awkward spots in the course of my wretched life but never have I been so looked down upon. What had I been doing with d'Indy? I had written such very charming things. But now? What's the good of it? How boring.

And now the youngsters are organising an anti-d'Indy movement and have played the *Sarabandes* and the *Fils des Etoiles* etc., works hitherto considered nothing but the product of ignorance, but now wrongly so, according to these people.

So that's what happens in life; it seems to have no sense whatever.

TO THE MAYOR OF ARCEUIL-CACHAN
Arceuil-Cachan, August 4th 1910

Dear Sir,

The District Council of Arceuil-Cachan is organising, as in preceding years, an outing for the school children who are breaking up. The number of children who will be able to take part in this nice excursion is restricted by reason of the Council's resources.

In order to forestall unfortunate disappointments for the children I have collected from among my friends and acquaintances a sum allowing me to offer a few children—a dozen, six girls and six boys—a pleasure they seldom have.

I beg your permission, Sir, to allow me to take out these twelve children I have chosen.

I enclose a list of the names of the children so that the masters and mistresses should not include them in their own lists. I shall have the consent of their parents and I undertake to be entirely responsible for these children entrusted to my care.

TO CONRAD SATIE
January 14th 1911

Here is a programme of the young composers. It contains a piece, much abbreviated, of your old brother.

And how are you? Ravel is a Rome prize-winner of very great talent. A Debussy *plus épatant*. He assures me every time I see him that he is greatly indebted to me. With which I am quite ready to agree. . . .

MÉMOIRES D'UN AMNÉSIQUE

Everyone will tell you that I am not a musician. (See Octave Séré: Musiciens français d'aujourd'hui, p. 138). This is quite right. From the beginning of my career I immediately ranked myself with the phonometrographers. My work is pure phonometry. Look at either the *Fils des Etoiles* or the *Morceaux en forme de poire* or *En habit de Cheval* or the *Sarabandes* and you will see that they are inspired by no kind of musical idea. They are the result of scientific thought.

I derive, moreover, more pleasure from measuring a sound than from listening to it. With my phonometer by me I work happily and securely.

What may I not thus have weighed and measured? The whole of Beethoven, the whole of Verdi and so on. And it is very strange.

The first time I used a phonoscope I examined a medium-sized B flat. I assure you that I have never seen anything so repulsive. I called in my servant to show it to him.

On the phono-weighing machine the ordinary F sharp, which we all know, registers as much as 93 kilogrammes. This was sung by a tremendously big tenor whose weight I noted.

Do you know about the cleaning of sounds? It's a rather dirty job. Spinning is cleaner. The job of putting sounds in order is very delicate and requires good eyesight. This brings us to the realm of phonotechnics.

In regard to sound explosions which are often unpleasant, cotton stuffed in the ears agreeably reduces the effect. Here we deal with pyrophony.

In writing my *Pièces froides* I used a recording caleidophone. It took seven minutes. I called in my servant to play them to him.

I think I may say that phonology is superior to music. It has more variety. And its financial return is greater. I have made my fortune from it.

In any case, at the monodynamophone a moderate use of the phonometer can easily produce more sounds than the most accomplished musician in the same time and with the same effort. It is thanks to this that I have written so much music.

The future thus lies with philophony.

(La Revue Musicale S.I.M., April 15th 1912)

TO VALENTINE HUGO

Arceuil, February 22nd 1915

Ma bonne Demoiselle,

I could jump for joy: I have just seen Jean Aubry who told me you were back. And how are you? And our publisher? And Madame? And the little girl?

I have become as silly as a goose; and I am eight months older. This war is upsetting me and turning me into a dreamer. I hope you are not affected by this abomination. . . .

May 16th 1916

Dear friend,

How goes it? I'm working like a horse and it's going better than I thought. May 30th at Bongard's is the "Granados-Satie" evening organised by Matisse, Picasso and others.

Bonjour très fort.

September 1916

Dear and sweet friend,

Very lovely your letter was—thank you. If you knew how sad I am. <i>Parade</i> is being transformed into something better <i>without</i> Cocteau. Picasso has ideas that appeal to me more than those of our Jean. And Cocteau doesn't know this. So what are we to do? Picasso tells me to go on with the scenario of Jean while he, Picasso, will work on another scenario of his own. It's staggering, wonderful! I'm crazy about it, but sad too. But there's nothing one can do. Knowing the beautiful conception of Picasso, I am distressed at having to compose to

the scenario of Jean which is decidedly less beautiful. What shall
I do? Write and advise me—I'm crazy about it.

(No date)

Dear Friend,

It's all arranged. Cocteau knows all about it. He and Picasso
are agreed. How lucky I am. . . . Did I tell you that I'm
getting on very well with Diaghilev? But still no money from
him. The "aunt" [Madame Edwards, patroness of Diaghilev]
is in Rum, I mean Rome.

January 6th 1917

I am now busy with the *Life of Socrates*. I am terrified of
making a mess of this work which I should like to reveal the
whiteness and purity of Antiquity. I am all of a dither and don't
know how to start. Beyond any doubt there is a beautiful
thing to be written on this idea. . . .

If I am "naughty" Montparnasse has nothing to do with it.
Life—not the Life of Socrates—is the reason. My "sister-in-
law" late Aunt Aubry, Debussy and others think that I am
under the influence of Montparnasse. They are to tell me what
to do, they alone. Which is about enough. . . .

January 18th 1917

What am I doing? I am working at the *Life of Socrates*. I
have found a fine translation, by Victor Cousin. Plato is a
wonderful collaborator, very sweet and discreet. So it's a
dream. I have written about it to the good Princess. I am swimming in happiness. I am free at last, free as the air, the water,
the wild sheep. Long live Plato! Long live Cousin! . . .

1918

Dear Valentine,

My suffering is too much. I have the feeling that I must be
cursed. This life of a beggar appals me.

I am looking for and would like to find a situation—a job, however small it may be. Art stinks; I've been fed up with it long enough. The job of an artist is lousy.

Forgive me, my dear friend, for using these true, these very true expressions. I'm writing to everyone. But no one replies— not even a friendly word. Dam' 'em!

You, my good friend, you who have always been good to your old friend, do see, I beg you, whether it wouldn't be possible to put him somewhere where he could earn his daily bread. Anywhere—I should not mind the most menial job I assure you. Do something about it quickly. I am at the end of my resources and can hold out no longer.

Art? For more than a month now I haven't written a note. I've not a single idea and I don't want to have any. Now what happens?

TO PIERRE BERTIN

(No date)

Here I was all by myself. Should have seen the sorry face I had. And no one to think of me except you and three hundred friends. And when I came home at night to my empty house, the piano just looked at me, the old thing—he didn't know.[1]

FROM A LECTURE GIVEN BY SATIE *c.* 1920

When I first met Debussy he was full of Moussorgsky and was very deliberately seeking a way that wasn't very easy to find. In this problem I was well in advance of him. I was not weighed down with the Prix de Rome, nor any other Prize, for I am a man like Adam (of Paradise) who never won any prizes—a lazy fellow, no doubt.

I was writing at that time *Le Fils des Etoiles* on a libretto by

---

[1] In its original Norman patois this is a most pathetic little note: "J'etaus ici, tout seul avec mi. Faudraut voir m'figure triste. Personne ne pensau à mi, sauf vous et trois cents amis. J'arrivau l'soir à m'maison, toute vide. L'piano m'regardant, l'pauvre fieu; il n's'avaut pas."

Joseph Péladan, and I explained to Debussy the need a French-man has to free himself from the Wagnerian venture, which didn't respond to our natural aspirations. I also pointed out that I was in no way anti-Wagnerian but that we should have a music of our own—if possible without any *Sauerkraut*.

Why could we not use the means that Claude Monet, Cézanne, Toulouse-Lautrec and others had made known? Why could we not transpose these means into music? Nothing simpler. . . .

That was the origin of a departure which brought results that were safe enough and even fruitful. Who was to show him examples? To reveal new treasures? To suggest the ground to be explored? To give him the benefit of previous considerations? Who? I shan't reply, for I no longer care.

APPENDIX A

HARRIET SMITHSON AND BERLIOZ[1]

Everyone who is at all acquainted with the life of Berlioz knows about Harriet Smithson, the famous Irish actress who was the inspiration of the *Symphonie Fantastique* and who, in 1833, became his wife. The biographers of Berlioz tell us that for three years (1820–30) he had been desperately in love with her without ever having met her. Then, suddenly, his passion is transferred to Camille Moke, and for Harriet, who in the role of Shakespeare's Juliet had fired the young Romantic's imagination to pathological limits, he has now only abuse. "I have no desire for vengeance," he writes to a friend. "I pity and despise her. She is but an ordinary type of woman, endowed with an instinctive power of expressing those pangs of the human soul which she has never felt, and incapable of entertaining a grand and noble sentiment such as that with which I have endowed her." Two years later, however, Berlioz was presented to her, and in October of the following year they were married at the British Embassy in Paris. Their married life lasted nine years.

This is a brief summary of the information to be obtained in the biographies of Berlioz, and which is based on his memoirs and correspondence. The story from Harriet Smithson's viewpoint, however, has not been told, and probably never will be, at least in its entirety, for first-hand documents on her life are extremely scarce, and those that are available throw little light on her relationship with Berlioz. Still, it is strange that no one has investigated her life beyond the account in the *Dictionary of National Biography*, for there are other sources, some of which will elucidate a point or two in the story as we know it.

The first thing that strikes us is that Harriet Smithson had a much smaller reputation as an actress in England than in France.

[1] First published in the *Musical Times*, December 1938, under the title "Unpublished Letters of Harriet Smithson and Berlioz", by the author.

Her success in the Shakespeare plays at the Odéon—the very performances which so impressed Berlioz—was, in her career, something quite exceptional. In Cumberland's *British Theatre* (vol. VII) we read that her appearances in Paris were "crowned with rapturous applause', but this fact, says the writer, "may easily be accounted for, since the French critics never saw Miss O'Neill and can have no conception of Siddons". And in Oxberry's *Dramatic Biography* (vol. II): "Miss Smithson would be a first-rate actress in a moderate-sized theatre—she has all the requisites to become so; at Drury Lane she is not one. To us it appears that Miss Smithson's greatest drawback is a want of confidence in her own powers, and, *perhaps*, their actual misapplication." Berlioz was often puzzled by her not wanting to return to England. The reason was simple enough: not only was her standing on this side of the Channel distressingly low, but there was apparently a strong, hostile feeling of jealousy that almost forbade her return. On this point the *Dictionary of National Biography* is explicit: "The announcement of her marriage in the Court Journal is ungraciously coupled with the expression of a wish that the marriage would prevent her reappearance on the English boards. . . . English opinion was almost uniformly hostile to her and even attributed her accident[1] to a theatrical ruse."

These contemporary accounts are all ungrudging, however, in their tributes to her beauty, and also to her morals. Oxberry, with extreme Victorian propriety, notes: "In private life, Miss Smithson need not blanch from investigation. Her conduct has been one continued and undeviating line of rectitude. Beautiful beyond the common run of beauty, yet as virtuous as beautiful; affable to all the members of the theatre, servile to none; *she* has never *coquetted* a manager into favour, nor marted her feelings for the sake of her interest." And there follow some anonymous "Stanzas on Miss Smithson," very much of the same period:

> "Can all be dark that life supplies
> Whilst earth can boast of Smithson's eyes?"

Beautiful—but very impecunious. She first appeared on an

[1] Shortly before her marriage, Harriet Smithson broke her leg as she stepped out of her carriage.

English stage at seventeen, in Birmingham. The following year she
appeared at Drury Lane in a play called *The Falls of Clyde*. At
twenty-four she was engaged by her brother at the English theatre
at Boulogne, where an important benefit performance was arranged
for her. One has the impression that henceforth a benefit performance was arranged for her in almost every town she visited. Her
appearances with Kemble and Macready at the Odéon were a
financial success, but her subsequent appearances in Paris were all
complete failures. True, she was unlucky. Her own season at the
Théâtre Italien in 1832 left her in debt to the extent of 14,000 francs,
and her engagement in the dumb rôle of Caecilia, in *L'Auberge
d'Auray*, a play with music by Hérold and Carafa, at the Opéra-
Comique in 1830, was never paid for. On this occasion she wrote the
following beseeching letter, hitherto unpublished, to no one less
than the King, Louis-Philippe himself. It is written in English and
dated August 15th, 1830, little less than four months before the
first performance of the *Symphonie Fantastique*.[1]

"Sire,
    "May it please your most gracious majesty to extend your
benignity and goodness in behalf of a Female, a foreigner who
ventures to make her humble complaint to your Majesty in the
simple words of truth, with the confidence that your Majesty'
heart will be the best intercessor in her favour.
    "Sire, at the repeated salutations of Col. Ducis and Mons. St.
St. Georges, the late directors of the Opéra-Comique, I was induced
five months since to accept an engagement to fulfil which I have
travelled one thousand miles accompanied by an aged mother and
an invalid sister both of whom are, and have been from my very
childhood solely dependent upon my professional exertions for
support. After having succeeded in my humble efforts and thereby

1 The manuscript of this letter is in the British Museum (Add. 33965, f. 89).
Other letters of Harriet Smithson are in the Conservatoires of Brussels (to
Mme Malibran) and Paris (to the Count d'Agoult). Both of these are
reproduced in Julien Tiersot's "Lettres de musiciens écrites en français"
(Vol. II, Paris, 1936). The catalogue of the Berlioz Exhibition held at
Frankfort in 1901 contains a letter from her dated October 31st, 1832.
Finally, J. Tiersot's "Le Musicien errant" contains a letter from Harriet
Smithson to her son, dated October 22nd, 1846.

considerably added to the treasury of the above named Gentlemen on applying for my hard-earned salary I discover'd they had both disappear'd, having spent in the most extravagant luxury the produce of my labours, without paying to me any part of the debt which their own signatures in my possession acknowledge as just. I have been now five months in Paris, I have sought justice in vain until it pleas'd God to give me sufficient courage to implore it at the fountain head, namely Your Majesty, to whom I would not address myself had I ever step'd aside from the path of rectitude which is the best recommendation misfortune can have. May it please Your Majesty I was inform'd on application at the Minister's of the interior by his representative that he would not grant the privilege for re-opening the Opéra-Comique until the debts due to the Artists were paid by the new Director. Yet the Theatre has been re-opened, some of the actors have been paid—but I, having no Father or Brother to protect me am denied my just claim 7,000.400 francs[1] earned at the expense of my health from over exertion, and the loss of my time for five months—one word from your most gracious Majesty to Mons. Guizot the *present* Minister who has I am told at his disposal the funds connected with the Theatres, would obtain for me the debt and dry the tears of an afflicted family in a strange Country who would pray to God to give your gracious Majesty that reward which is the brightest hope in this transitory life.

"With the greatest deference I have the honour to subscribe myself
          "Sire
                    "Your Majesty's most humble & obedient Servant
                              "Harriet C. Smithson.
"Rue de Rivoli 44
"Hotel du Congress."[2]

It was Berlioz's passion for Shakespeare that first attracted him to Harriet Smithson; and this passion remained with him till the end

---

[1] She means, of course, 7,400 francs.

[2] Above the letter is written in French: "Miss Smithson requests that the Minister of the Interior pay her the sum owed to her by the former directors of the Opéra-comique." And in another hand: "The Minister has no money for this purpose."

of his life. We have evidence of this from another unpublished letter in the British Museum, from Berlioz to the Dutch musician, Edward Silas. At least it would appear to be evidence, for only the most ardent Shakespearian could be so critical of Racine as Berlioz is in this letter. The addressee, Edward Silas (1827–1909), was a teacher at the Guildhall School of Music, the composer of numerous songs and piano pieces, a symphony, and an oratorio, *Joash*, produced at the Norwich Festival of 1863 and dedicated to Berlioz. The letter, here translated, is doubtless written in acknowledgment of this dedication:

                                                  January 6th, 1864
"My dear Silas,
    "I am still unwell. However, this morning M. Paque[1] came to see me and we spoke for a long time about you. He had the most complimentary things to say about your oratorio. I had already an excellent opinion of it, having read it through carefully many times. You cannot imagine the trouble I have had reading a score engraved with those frightful English notes which would put any music out of shape and make it look heavy. Also I find the characters of your Sacred Drama extremely unpleasant. I have a horror of them from the tragedy of Racine[2]—a work that people in France call a masterpiece. I have no love nor hate for Athalie, but I loathe that crazy Joad whom the English so amusingly call Jehoiada, and especially that foul little Joas with his sanctified air and his silly smirk. In spite of all this, your work contains a host of very lovely things— for instance, the trio, "There is in him a charm", the March of the Levites and the Chorus of the Baalites which, with a good choir singing with life, should produce a fine effect. The lines of Joas, "Teach me O Lord!" are very graceful, and you were actually able to write some interesting music for that pompous chorus of praise, 'Come let me praise the Lord with joy!'"
    Berlioz then points out a printer's error, and concludes:
    "Let me present my sincere compliments. Unfortunately I have not a score of *Les Troyens* to send you. My publisher gave me a

---

[1] Guillaume Paque (1825–76), a well-known Belgian 'cellist who established a reputation in London.
[2] *Athalie.*

M

certain number of copies, which promptly disappeared from my
house, and I cannot ask him for any more. But if I get another
copy I will send it to you.
                    "Farewell,
                        "In friendship,
                              "H. Berlioz."

The second part of *Les Troyens* had been given the previous year,
but the work in its entirety was not to be heard until twenty-one
years after the composer's death. *Joash* has not been heard since the
Norwich performance of 1863.

APPENDIX B

LETTER FROM EMMANUEL CHABRIER TO HIS WIFE

This letter, the longest of the published letters of Chabrier, displays his literary gifts in the most vivid manner. In her recent publication of it in La Revue de Musicologie, *Madame Paul-Marie Masson does not overstate its value in describing it as "a real masterpiece showing us in Chabrier the jester and the philosopher, the musician and the painter, the dramatist and the humourist". Because of its unusual interest I have thought it appropriate to set it apart here as an envoi.[1]*

TO MADAME CHABRIER

Mont-Dore, August 15th, 1891

Maman. . . . I want to tell you about two excursions I have been on; the last four or five days the weather has been glorious, blue everywhere and very warm. Here it's one thing or the other. The day before yesterday Madame Abry and her son—the Firmins had gone off early in the morning on another jaunt—Madame Abry, my friend who has always got something wrong with her, arrived at about 8 in the morning—I was correcting proofs in my room— said that the weather was wonderful and that she'd be very glad if I'd go on an outing with her. I was delighted to accept, particularly because she wanted to show her appreciation of my having played, as she had asked me to, at the local chemist's, another very nice fellow who supplies me with things I need for nothing. So off we went, the three of us, Madame Abry, her son and me; this son of hers is fourteen but he looks eighteen; he gives himself airs and thinks himself a character—he's an extraordinary type of *fin-de-siècle* person. The country is *wonderful*; less majestic than Cauterets where you can't move without knocking into a terrific mountain that blocks the view, but it's dramatic all right and it's utterly delightful. The Mont-Dore is of course in the valley surrounded by

[1] I am greatly indebted to M. Oswald d'Estrade-Guerra of the Bibliothèque Nationale for kindly having drawn my attention to this document.

high mountains each with a name of its own, a little story, a pretty
waterfall, its vale of death and so on, and of which the highest is
the Pic de Sancy which you see from everywhere around. . . . The
carriage went up and up and then suddenly—I'm still speaking of
the day before yesterday—I came up against a wonderful panorama
which struck me as all the more beautiful since Madame Abry had
said nothing about it, wanting to see how surprised I was going to
be. At the top of the hill—imagine that we were 5000 ft. above sea-
level—I see in front of me two enormous rocks rising from nowhere
and standing up there like gigantic Pyramids, two sentinels of
Nature keeping guard on the vast stretch of country, and this
country stretching out to the horizon was of every colour, purple,
pink, green like the waves of the sea; and all this was gilded and lit
up by the burning sun. I have never seen anything more beautiful.
At six in the evening we returned to the Mont-Dore. But it was
yesterday we had the loveliest excursion. The Firmins, who also
wanted to be nice to me, insisted on our leaving at 7 in the morning.
In the landau there were Antoinette, the two Firmins, the young
Abry and myself. After being on the way for four hours, climbing
up 8 miles of terrible roads and then spending an hour coming
down, we arrived at 11 at the Château de Murols. I shall come back
to this—but these mountains which our carriage wound around
appeared to change their appearance at every moment and so we
were all the time presented with a new view. The horse trotted
along at tremendous heights, the mountains on the left, a precipice
on the right, and then we came down about a 1000 ft in zigzags, in
hairpin bends with waterfalls on the way, terrifying mountain
torrents, pinewoods rushing at us and seeming to fall right down on
us—*I really didn't know where I was.* I've never seen anything more
beautiful in my life, and all the time I kept muttering, If only my
sweet little thing were with me, if only she were, if only she were;
you would have been absolutely in raptures, my sweet, and in fact
although I was overjoyed at this sight I was all the same saddened at
the thought of this wonder which you were not sharing. But don't
be too annoyed with me, my love. Well, here we were at the Château
or rather at the foot of the Château de Murols; Murols is a dincky
little village on the side of a lake surrounded of course by mountains, for all these lakes are situated at terrific heights; and this lake

was so calm, you could see right to the bottom. Then we climbed to
the Château, completely in ruins but wonderfully interesting. It
dates from 1350 and belonged to two families, Murols and d'Estaing.
It took 200 years to build and in the Revolution of 89 it was
destroyed in ten minutes. This castle is on a vast scale, but there are
now only remains of the cross-bridges, the machiolated gateways
and windows; but when you go inside there are chunks of gilded
columns and tops of coloured doors and mantelpieces which show
how magnificent this dwelling must have been. There is a postern
high up and I will let you imagine the *stupendous* view you have
from there! And then what the sight of this enormous jagged shell
of a castle so marvellously conveys is what it must have been like
in feudal times, with battles engaged upon and waged, with the
holes through which the archers poured boiling oil and other
horrors on to the cross-bowmen below—all the ridiculous hulla-
baloo in fact that you must have seen as a child in the historical plays
that used to be given at the Porte Saint-Martin, as I did too. After
having slipped a coin to the old lady dressed up in period clothes
who had gone through her rigmarole, we went down to Murols
where in the landau we retraced our road back to St Nectaire
arriving at 12.15 absolutely ravenous. . . .

At St. Nectaire there is a spa well known round about here for
women's diseases; there are very few people there—only ten women
and girls, jaundiced and cadaverous with thick greenish lips and
clammy hands—you can see what this amounts to—ten such
females for one gouty, swollen-necked and scurvey old boy. My
whole life I've heard of St. Nectaire, but I can't see any future for it,
for the roads leading to it are terrible though absolutely wonderful,
and that's of course why we went. But it isn't worth the candle.
But the view is astounding! There is the very interesting old
Romanesque church perched on a mountain 300 ft. up and you get
to it up a very gentle slope. The inside is very well preserved, but
these Romanesque churches are nothing but stone, and there is
never the slightest little amusing piece of ornamentation. You can
imagine that I wanted to see the curé—he was there all right and
soon turned up, his face beaming all over. He was a fellow I could
get on with. He came from a district very near Ambert, he asked
me my name and it wasn't five minutes before we were larking

about like two magpies. You're sure enough from Auvergne, he said. Why, you are a Chevalier of the Légion d'Honneur! Wonderful! He pushed a tract on the church into my hand, was dying to write his name on it and I slipped a two-franc piece into my old compatriot's withered hand for the dear old poor. I think he would have canonised me! Then we took the road down, and to make a short cut to the hotel we had to climb down an extremely steep hill and I will now tell you that I negotiated this most admirably. Antoinette had her skirt pulled half way up her legs, and so did Marguerite and they were both in a fix for young Abry, who isn't yet fifteen but clever as a monkey kept on prowling round taking a peep at their naked legs or picking up one of their garters; the little devil made a great nuisance of himself but we couldn't help laughing! Firmin wanted to go down upright; he kept on slipping and sprawling and when he finally got up he slipped again and gave it up. But as for me—I of course saw immediately what was to be done. I don't know what I should have been like going up, but going down I won the prize: I just squatted down on my behind, the grass was dry and warm, I turned sideways pushing myself with my right hand and grabbing a tuft of grass when I felt I was going too quickly. After a moment I stood up to see which way I should proceed, but all of a sudden—plomp! I found myself on my behind again, and this time down I went the hill rolly-polly, just avoiding some rocks on the way, until I got to the main road—the others were by this time far behind. Some passers-by, very distinguished people who were quite unknown to me, warmly congratulated me.

At last our retinue reformed and we got back to the hotel. I played some comic turns on the tinny drawing room piano for three ugly old ladies, and I played again on the way back for some pasty-faced young girls and also a schoolboy whose lips were like the edge of a chamber pot and who when he laughed, the wretch, disclosed a frightful gorilla jaw and enormous horse teeth and bleeding gums. I've seen two frights like this before, one was Edouard Dujardin, the former editor of *La Revue Wagnérinene* and the other was Benjamin Godard. This is the third, and I don't want to see any more! Then lemonade all round—a great effect this seemed to have on the ladies—and did I tell you that Firmin insisted on paying for everything; every time I offered to pay he just grabbed my purse and threw it on the floor. . . .

I could tell you many more things but I'd rather not write them; just wait till we are alone. Eventually the horses began to jingle their bells, we got into the carriage and we were off. We came back the same way, winding round the great mountains, the horse going slowly up the hills and trotting down the slopes. We saw the wonderful views again—you simply wouldn't have been able to tear yourself away from this spot from 7 in the morning till 8 at night—and we then wrapped ourselves in our coats, for it was gradually getting chilly, but only a little, and there were then the wonderful country smells of the newly-cut corn and these smells seemed to come from the open sea—they were so strong and penetrating; it was as if the whole perspiration of the earth on this hot day were reaching us. I cannot tell you what a lovely feeling this was; and on the mountain sides, as we passed them one after the other while evening drew in we saw vast herds of cows, almost all of them mahogany-coloured, forming ragged circles right from the peaks down to the valleys; from far away we heard the sounds of the little bells round their necks, all the same sounds but tinkling with strange little rhythms; and then the calls of the shepherds and their furious dogs racing through the immense stretches of pasture land, of a deeper green in patches now for night was falling; and then came the shepherd's cart made of pinewood with flowery wheels drawn by oxen and in which he actually sleeps—it may be an old shepherd or a young shepherd—under the stars and in all weather and absolutely alone and quiet, looking, looking—well, looking at what? At the most beautiful sights, the lucky devil. And there he sleeps, the young shepherd or the old one as the case may be, for eight to ten days at a time before bringing in his herd. No newspapers from Paris for him. Fate glues him to the contemplation of Nature's constantly renewed glories, and to be sure when one has seen such wonders one can only envy people who, without cares and worries, can look upon such things. They are the happy ones—obviously. Well, what's to be done about it? But then ultimately comes the winter with 40 to 50 ft. snow over the whole country. Not a single track in the snow can be made, not a journey, nothing at all. The houses, the humble cottages, the shepherd's cart, they are all fast asleep for six months—and woe to anyone who dare venture abroad; he would be lost at twenty feet from his house, and the long dangerous roads are studded with crosses where a traveller lost in the snow, overcome by a snowstorm has simply been smothered and crushed and hurled into the distance; a little white hole has been dug out for him and then more snow to stuff the little white hole up, and it's all over.

Well, what a yarn, as Mère Tonnelier would say, she who wouldn't give a damn for the Romanesque style or the shepherd's dogs—but what's happened to the dogs of Mère Gatien? And the canary you spoke to me about the other day? What—we have a canary? And by the way, please tell Marcel that when he uses the word cauterize, whether he's speaking of some smart woman or the biggest rogue, it's always spelt like that and not with an *o*. Thank him for his letter with which I was delighted—and I hope he goes on studying in earnest. He'll get to the end of his work one of these days, but he's not there yet, nor am I, though I am 33 years older than he and I'm beginning to wonder whether my turn will ever come. . . .

More details tomorrow. Try and take a brandy to digest all this. Love to you all—Yes, Great God! and a hearty kiss, my sweet wife from

> Your pet,
> Emmanuel.

BIBLIOGRAPHY

BERLIOZ, Hector

Correspondance inédite (1819–1868). Paris, 1879.

Lettres intimes. Paris, 1882.

3 vols. of Letters edited by Julien Tiersot, Paris, 1904–30:

   Vol. I—*Les Années romantiques (1819–42)*

   Vol. II—*Le Musicien errant (1842–52)*

   Vol. III—*Au milieu du chemin (1852–55)*.

Briefe an die Fürstin Carolyn Sayn-Wittgenstein, edited by La Mara. Leipzig, 1903.

BIZET, Georges

Lettres de Georges Bizet: Impressions de Rome (1857–1860);
La Commune (1871). Preface by Louis Ganderax. Paris, 1907.
Lettres à un ami (1865–1872). Introduction by Edmond Galabert. Paris, 1909.

CHABRIER, Emmanuel

Le don Chabrier à la Bibliothèque Nationale. By Renée Girardon.
La Revue de Musicologie. Paris, Nouvelle série, XXVIIe Année, Nos. 74-75, 2e-3e Trimestre 1945; XXVIIIe Année, Nos. 77-78, 1er-2e Trimestre 1946.
Chabrier d'après ses lettres. L'homme et l'oeuvre. By Joseph Désaymard. Paris, 1934.

DEBUSSY, Claude

Lettres de Claude Debussy à son éditeur (i.e. Jacques Durand). Paris, 1927.
Correspondance de Claude Debussy et Paul-Jean Toulet. Paris, 1929.
La Jeunesse de Pelléas: Lettres de Claude Debussy à André Messager. Paris, 1938.

Lettres de Claude Debussy à deux amis (Robert Godet and G. Jean-Aubry). Paris, 1942.
Correspondance de Claude Debussy et Pierre Louÿs (1893–1904). Recueillie et annotée par Henri Borgeaud. Paris, 1945.
Debussy et d'Annunzio: Correspondance inédite. Présentée par Guy Tosi. Paris, 1948.
Lettres inédites à André Caplet (1908–14). Recueillies et présentées par Edward Lockspeiser. Paris, 1957.
Lettres de Claude Debussy à sa femme Emma. Présentées par Pasteur Vallery-Radot. Paris, 1957.

FAURÉ, Gabriel
Lettres intimes. Présentées par Philippe Fauré–Frémiet. Paris, 1951.
Lettres à sa fiancée (i.e. Marianne Viardot). Présentées par Camille Bellaigne. Revue des deux mondes. Paris, August 15th 1928.

PINCHERLE, Marc
Musiciens peints par eux-mêmes. Lettres de compositeurs écrites en français (1771–1910). Paris, 1939.

RAVEL, Maurice
Ravel au miroir de ses lettres. Correspondance réunie par Marcelle Gérar et René Chalupt. Paris, 1956.
"Letters to M. D. Calvocoressi." *The Musical Quarterly*, New York, January, 1941
"Lettres de Maurice Ravel et documents inédits". By Roland-Manuel. *Revue de Musicologie*. Paris, Vol. XXXVIII. July 1956.

SAINT-SAËNS, Camille
Portraits et Souvenirs. Paris, 1908 (?).
Harmonie et Mélodie. Paris, 1923.

SATIE, Erik

"Erik Satie: son temps et ses amis". Special number of *La Revue Musicale* published under the editorship of Rollo Myers. Paris, June 1952.
Erik Satie, by Rollo H. Myers. London, 1948.
Erik Satie, by Pierre-Daniel Templier. Paris 1952.

TIERSOT, Julien.
Lettres de Musiciens écrites en français du XVe au XXe siècle. Vol. I (de 1480 à 1830). Vol. II (de 1831 à 1885). Turin and Paris, 1924.

INDEX